A LE[barcode] BY THE INDUS

MEMORIES OF MIGRANTS
FROM
DERA ISMAIL KHAN

ARUNA KOHLI

INDIA • SINGAPORE • MALAYSIA

Notion Press Media Pvt Ltd

No. 50, Chettiyar Agaram Main Road,
Vanagaram, Chennai, Tamil Nadu – 600 095

First Published by Notion Press 2021
Copyright © Aruna Kohli 2021
All Rights Reserved.

ISBN
Hardcase: 978-1-63904-632-4
Paperback: 978-1-63886-524-7

Dedicated
to
My Parents

Contents

Preface

This book is by no means a complete repository of the oral culture of the Hindu migrants from Dera Ismail Khan. It is a humble effort to retrieve as much as I could before it fades into oblivion. This is a tribute to the Saraiki speaking elders who crossed over to India in 1947 and to those who perished while doing so. It is an expression of gratitude to honour the memories of those valiant men and women who rebuilt their lives for themselves and their forbears braving all odds. The intention is to document an unwritten culture and a language which is on the verge of extinction in India where those who know it crave to speak but there is nobody around. This work may enable future generations to peek into their roots as well as serve as an interesting resource for researchers.

I thank my family for supporting and encouraging me by going all out to contribute by way of recollections of their home-town, DI Khan. Phone calls spread sheer joy to everyone I contacted both in India and abroad. Memories have become faint for many but the very idea of a book became a tool to reconnect with those who were virtually lost from my immediate horizon.

I am grateful to the following people for their precious time and valuable inputs by way of information.

1. Col. P.C. Sethi (Retd.)
2. Shri Subhash Chander Sachdeva
3. Smt. Pramil Sachdeva
4. Shri O.P. Sachdeva (Pretam)

5. Shri S.P. Sethi (Ram)
6. Smt. Sarla Menon
7. Shri. Ashok Dhingra
8. Shri Chander Dhingra
9. Shri Mahesh Chander Sachdeva
10. Smt. Kamal Grover
11. Smt. Rita Sethi
12. Dr. Renuka Sethi
13. Smt. Swaran Palta
14. Smt. Saroj Kumar
15. Smt. Minnie Kandhari
16. Smt. Beeta Mehta
17. Shri Sudhir Manchanda
18. Dr. Neeraj Sethi
19. Shri Arun Sethi
20. Smt. Isha Sachdeva

Photographs courtesy:

Smt.Chanderkanta Kumar, Smt. Rita Sethi, Shri S.C. Sachdeva, Anita Sachdeva, Smt. Usha Verma, Shalini Sethi, Smt. Prabha Sachdeva, Dr. S.S. Sachdeva, Smt. Beeta Mehta, Shri Sudhir Manchanda, Shri Ashok Dhingra, Shri Chander Dhingra, Dr. Neeraj Sethi, Smt. Uma Ahuja, Smt. Mala Kapur.

COVER DESIGN: Asha Kohli Sethi

Chapter 1

A Heritage

Calcutta 1957: A house, next to the noisy tram depot, in Gariahat Road resounded with Khwaja Ghulam Farid's song *"Peelu Pakiyaan Vey"* sung with great passion by two stalwarts from pre-partition Dera Ismail Khan. They were my father, Dr. Lachhman Das Sachdeva and his friend, Dr. Chetan Lal Piplani. This was my earliest memory of a culture that was to be unravelled at various stages of my growing years. The flashback is crystal clear and my cultural journey begins hereon as a six year old. Ever since then Dera Ismail Khan holds a certain mystique. I can only visualise their ancestral home town, a forlorn memory for its Hindu residents who had to move out en masse seeking new beginnings. They found solace in each other's presence, spoke their mother tongue Derewali, regaling each other with shared memories and trying to reconnect with common friends. I have known them to be warm hearted, affectionate and overly hospitable.

Years have flown by with struggles, challenges, growing up and settling down in a new locale. Today, the scene seems almost empty as most of the key players have departed leaving behind an invaluable legacy. My father descended the stage on February 5, 2015 after 96 years. He enriched our lives with a culture he unknowingly passed on. He would traverse long distances to meet literally the who's-who of his home town and introduce them to us. Shri Tek Chand Dhingra, the freedom fighter, in Kankhal, Hardwar, Shri Atamchand Piplani in Meerut, Shri Jyot Singh Mongia, Dr. R.L. Soota, Shri Lekhraj Ailawadi and his father,

Shri Jaswant Ram Ailawadi, who edited an Urdu magazine in Dehra Dun and authored the book 'Hamara Dera Ismail Khan—Tasveer-e-Ashiana', Shri Jaidayal Gadi and Shri D.B. Shyam Khattar were some familiar faces we have seen as children. We met them in passing but now feel the significance of those meetings which were a part of our roots. They opened their eyes in Dera Ismail Khan on the western banks of the river Indus (better known to them as Sindh Dariya) to a post-World War I scenario of scarcities and instabilities. Their childhood, youth and adolescence was sandwiched between World Wars I and II followed by the partition of undivided India.

As trouble fanned the fires which blazed across the bazaars of Dera Ismail Khan these brave hearts fled from the very land their forefathers guarded and survived in the face of carnage and onslaught of foreign invaders. But this time it was a mass exodus no one could stop. These resilient men and women have since lived their dreams and made safe havens for their offspring. Most of them have departed but for the few who remain it is late autumn and a tottering and laboured existence. Their language Derewali is a dying language on this side of the border and their cultural legacy will soon be a faint memory.

The city, Dera Ismail Khan derives its name from a Baluchi chieftain Ismail Khan who settled here and founded the old city in 1469. Ismail Khan was the son of a Baloch mercenary Malik Sohrab Dodai. Sultan Husain, the Langah king of Multan handed over control of his trans-Indus territories to Malik Sohrab Dodai as a *jagir*. Malik Sohrab Dodai's sons, Ismail Khan and Fateh Khan founded the two Deras (settlements) named after them. Ismail Khan's descendants ruled the city for 300 years.

Dera Ismail Khan, also known as *"Dera Phullan Da Sehra"* (crown of flowers), has been aptly described by James Howard Thornton in his book[1] "Memories of Seven Campaigns" (1895)__"A considerable native town adjoins the cantonment, and both are surrounded by a beautiful circular road, planted on each side with fine trees forming a shady avenue. The roads through the station and its vicinity are excellent and well kept, and there are some pretty public gardens." However, a stark contrast to this description is L.A. Starr's impression in her book[2] "Frontier Folk of the Afghan Border and Beyond" (1920) where she mentions the town popularly known to the British as "Dreary Dismal". Count Hans Von Koenigsmarck's impression[3] of DI Khan, "....the abomination of desolation red-hot in summer, bitterly cold in winter" is mentioned in his book,'A German Staff Officer in India'. In John Travers's book[4], 'Sahib Log', Esme, General Norman's wife, describes her journey as "the long strange journey, the primitive tonga drive, and the weird Bridge of Boats." The January-June 1915 issue of Black Wood's magazine[5], despite its unflattering comments about the town, admits, "The people of Dera are indeed fine fellows. The main charm of the place then lies in the people." Derewals are a simple, affectionate, hardworking community genetically possessing a high cerebral quotient. The Hindu and Sikh inhabitants left the town which once reverberated with laughter, festivities, beliefs and an aeons old lifestyle and unwritten culture which existed along the Indus river.

While re-tracing the steps of my parents during my research I discovered the above extract of Thornton which, I presume, was the Mall Road often alluded to as the *"Thandi Sarak"* (cool street) by them. The cantonment, I am told, had the *"Jarnaili Bangla"*(General's or GOC's bungalow) owned by my paternal grandfather, Lala Neb Raj Sachdeva. On the vast grounds of the bungalow there had been a girl-guides event in which my mother participated as a school-girl singing *"Main Hun Neeli Chidiya"* (I am a blue bird). The GOC's bungalow fetched them a monthly rent of Rs.100/-. Initially the bungalow had a joint owner, Shri Sidhu Ram Dhingra, who had one-third share but later it was bought over totally by my grandfather. My father recalled his house in Topawala Bazaar which had a jamun tree and saplings of grapes, transported all the way from Quetta. These grew to bear juicy fine quality fruit. The wooden gate of the 'Jha' or house was burnt by a mob which was not allowed to enter the premises by the house-keeper Allah Baksh. They spewed the ultimate insult of a '*kafir*' (infidel) but unmindful of this Allah Baksh stood as a sentinel, guarding the property of his employer who was away in Burma. A strong iron gate was installed after his return from Burma.

Chapter 2

The Patriarch

Lala Neb Raj Sachdeva

Mounted atop a wall his gaze was rather severe and sent a chill down our spine, we his grand-children, he had never known. The photographers of those days could never make their subjects smile. Black and white photos hold a certain charm and this visage of my grandfather, Lala Neb Raj Sachdeva was endowed with a morphed crown upon his head by the lop-sided artistic sense of the photographer. His face belied his gentle disposition. He was a landlord who owned a village called Garha Chheena. The village, owned by the family, also had a red-light area rentals from which ranged between Rs.3 to Rs.7 and were collected by Allah Baksh, their trusted employee. The silver coins from occupants of the red-light area were cleansed before being handed over to the family. During the harvest season sacks of wheat were sent on camel-driven carts to the market. Seeds were given by the landlord and half the harvested crop was shared with the labourers. The village was sold to Shri Basant Lal Malik much before the partition.

Being a compulsive shopaholic, grandfather would impulsively buy a whole stable of horses only to be chided by his wife. At one of the auctions he bought a complete library with furniture and housed it in his bungalow, *'Jha'*. This was the beginning of my father's voracious reading habit and quest for knowledge. As a young boy he had his own private library with encyclopaedia, biographies, classics and complete works of famous English authors. On another occasion, he brought home an evening gown for 'Kaki', his very cloistered and traditional eldest daughter-in-law. Needless to say it was never worn. The *'Jha'* was a treasure trove for Lachhman Das, my father, to explore as a school boy. Lodged in one of the rooms was an antique harmonium or *'Peti'* which had foot pumps and could be played with both hands. My father mastered it as a school boy and became a self-taught musician. The *'Jha'* was a feast for the discerning viewer as it was furnished with antique furniture, artistic lamps and chandeliers and collector's pieces bought from auctions. After grandfather died the house was rented by Mr Memon, an Oxford educated gentleman who was highly appreciative of the fine aesthetic sense of its owner. Adjoining the *'Jha'* grandfather built an Eye Hospital for his eldest son Dr. Dukhbhanjan Lal. It was well equipped and had a sign-board which read *"Gareebon Ke Liye Muft Ilaaj"* (Free treatment for the poor).

Many years later, in the summer of 1960 we encountered two blue eyed fair sardars with snow-white beards in Simla. They seemed like ethereal beings dropped from above. Their eyes lit up at the mere mention of my grandfather's name for they were none other than his auctioneers who had set up a small stall selling foreign goods and cosmetics

Chapter 3

Hindon River Flood

The year 1947 saw a miraculous saga unfold. The doctor, Lachhman Das Sachdeva, enlisted in the British-Indian Army had to give his preference for the country of his choice. Without batting an eye he opted for the country of his birthplace never realising the gravity of the situation. As he set off westwards his journey was stalled by a mighty flood on the river Hindon. The waters did not recede for the next three days. The Hindon river deluge was Godsent and decided his fate or else he would have been separated forever from his kith and kin and fiancée, Vimla, who had crossed over to India. A telegram arrived informing him of the cross-over of his family during his halt at Hindon. He re-united with his family at Jullundar, where he was posted, and a joyous wedding was arranged at his cousin, Capt.Thakur Das Sachdeva's house where his fiancée, was staying. On April 9, 1948, a pandit solemnised the nuptials. The baraat or wedding procession was *sans* a musical band but with music from a gramophone record. The *doli* or departure of the bride took place with an improvised fanfare and clanging of *thalis* or metal plates with ladles. It was a small gathering of close relatives on the lawns of Capt. T.D. Sachdeva's bungalow in Jullundar Cantonment. The wedding feast was catered by Chamier's Hotel. The groom's colleagues at the army hospital were not invited as he was marrying a refugee girl and did not wish to burden the bride's mother with too many guests.

Chapter 4

A Flashback

The year 1968 in Dehra Dun revived distant memories. He was my father's golf-companion and friend, a retired Brigadier, wizened with a receding hairline. Some faces cannot be easily forgotten. The dotted lines of the past do meet sometime, somewhere. The person who confronted my maternal grandmother, Daya Vati Sethi (wife of Late Dr. Milap Chand Sethi) brought a whiff of the 1947 air which reverberated with the slogan "Captain Tandon Zindabad". It was a fateful meeting with their hero, Brig Tandon, who brought their refugee train safely across the border.

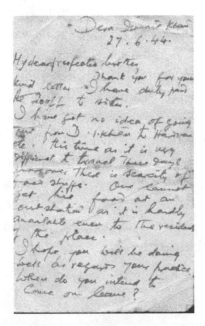

Letter written by Dr.Milap Chand Sethi depicting the hardships of war time.

Dr. Milap Chand Sethi, renowned physician of DI Khan.

Dr. Milap Chand Sethi, my maternal grandfather, passed away a year before partition at 39 years of age. A year later, his young wife, Daya Vati left the comfort and safety of her home to travel eastwards and confront an uncertain future with her teenaged daughter and three sons still in school. They travelled one fateful day of April 1947 from Dera Ismail Khan to Rawalpindi from where they boarded a train to Chaklala after the 15th of August. An accident, further down the track, hampered their movement on the second day and their refugee train was offloaded in Sialkot. They camped in barracks and washed themselves at an old horse's moat. Food supplies were frugal and measured portions were distributed. Their diet comprised two chappaties per adult and one per child along with some runny *dal* (lentil). Her boys were ever hungry and Daya Vati had carried two large tins of '*mathis*' (crisp deep-fried flour pancakes) and '*tosha*' (sugar-coated fried flour-dough squares). Before they could partake of the snacks the boxes vanished along with a trunk-load of clothes. The little boys would sneak out of the camp, impersonating as Muslims, to buy something to slay their hunger.

Once their train journey resumed, heavy trunks with all their worldly possessions were loaded by Ved, Daya Vati's 12 year old son, as coolies had surged their rates to Rs.5/-per box. Their onward journey from Sialkot to Lahore was at snail's pace and took them five days. They could hear sniper shots at Lahore. It was a packed train. They slept over their trunks which were mounted one atop the other just short of the roof of the train. Prayers were their only recourse. "*Bole So Nehal, Sat Sri Akal*" was said in hushed tones.

Chapter 5

Early Memories

Childhood in DIKhan. (L to R) Siblings Lachchman Das and Harikrishan Sachdeva.

At V.B. High School, salwar-kurta was the dress-code of this boys school where initial years were spent writing on 'takhtis'or wooden boards with 'kalam' or wooden pens. The heavily flared salwar was too much for a small boy to handle in school that he would wait outside his elder brother's class room to have it fastened after a visit to the rest-room. The class teacher patiently permitted these frequent daily interruptions. Lachhman Das, my father, proudly donned his Frontier salwar-kurta throughout his college years at Forman Christian College and King Edward Medical College, Lahore. At one of the annual functions of the medical college, he was given a thunderous applause and a mention in the front page column of the Times of India for his rendition of K.L. Sahgal's *"Suno Suno Re Krishan Kala...."*

A good boy was one who fared well in academics and grew up to be a doctor, engineer or college professor. Lachhman Das fell into the category of a good boy. Spoiled by an exemplary school record of consistent high scores he took the liberty of coining a pseudonym for himself in a moment of mischief at the examination hall. He excelled in Urdu, the answer paper was well-done and he was the teacher's favourite student so he thought he could indulge in some harmless prank. With a glint in his eye he calligraphed the name "*Gadbad Jhangi Ram*" and eagerly awaited the results. "Of course", he felt, "the teacher would just laugh at the prank played by his favourite student. He could not possibly be reprimanded for a paper which was well done." The D-day arrived. Answer papers were handed out and marks announced. The Urdu school master had one paper firmly lodged under his armpit. Lachhman Das waited for the big laugh. The master announced, "*Gadbad Jhangi Ram*", pointedly looked at him and called him in front of the class. What followed next was a loud crackling smack never to be forgotten for a lifetime. His examination hall tomfoolery did not end there but became more imaginative as he inked a vertical line in the last sentence of his answer paper by pulling the sheet upwards to give the impression of "I had more to write" if only the invigilator had not rudely snatched the answer paper. Learning English was every boy's aspiration. A poem, popular among the boys, was passed on and recited with a rhythmic beat,

"Pidgeon Kabootar
Udan Fly
Look Dekho
Asmaan Sky."

ZIG-ZAG MISCHIEF

Escorting his cloistered sister-in-law to her maternal home was my father's duty. At a young age of 12 he had often conducted the task dutifully. It was a mystery to the little boy how a veiled woman could see through her dupatta (scarf) and follow him. At short intervals he would glance back to check on her. Bored of this mundane routine he entertained himself with a few variations from the trodden path. He started walking a zig-zag trail across the road and was amused to glance back and check that his uncomplaining and much older sister-in-law silently vended the circuitous route through her veil without any deviations.

GROWING YEARS

Innocence and memories of childhood years were left behind somewhere by the Sindh dariya (Indus River) where they would splash and swim like there was no tomorrow. The Sindh dariya was the scene of social outings and recreation like '*Dhavni*' (swimming). A Derewal migrant poet, Kishan Chand Rahi, strikes a nostalgic chord in his verse,

"*Dhavni khoob manende husse*
Kaddu ban ke dhande husse
Naal churma khande husse
Puri kheer te pakvaan
Bhul nai sakda DI Khan"

Dhavni was a community bath by the river Indus where people would congregate and swim with a pumpkin fastened to their waists to keep afloat.

Those were the times when you couldn't ask a parent for money. A paisa meant the small joy of buying a sweetmeat or a '*sherbet-gola*' (ice-candy) but it was grudgingly handed out. "*Bhabhi paisa....*" Lachhman Das mumbled a scared whisper to his mother. No sooner had he uttered his request, the little boy heard a thunderous retort, "Whaaat" which sounded more like a deterrent than a question. That silenced him and he went his way dejected and dimeless. Most children were given money according to the whims of elders as it was considered a bad habit. Those were days of the gramophone which children nicknamed "*Kutta Baja*" (Dog's instrument) as HMV records had a dog for a logo. Lachhman Das's kid brother would belt out songs imitating a gramophone. His finger was the needle and his belly represented the round record. The finger would move as the song progressed from the edge of the belly towards the navel where it would end.

Ramchand, a childhood friend and tenant, introduced Lachhman Das to the fascinating world of magic in D I Khan. The sleight of hands and secret tips of a magician were imparted to him by his friend who became a professional magician and settled down in Jhansi where he opened a fabric store after the partition. In the mid 70s he resurfaced from the past, visited our home in Delhi and regaled us with an impromptu and improvised magic show with newspapers compressed into spherical shapes.

Two sons of the soil need mention. Professor Dinanath Baweja, the singer who became an All India Radio Artiste after partition and taught Hindustani classical music at his music school-cum-residence at Kalkaji for years. At a time when music as a career was unthinkable, Prof Dinanath was encouraged by his maternal uncle, Lala Tekchand Dhingra, who took the bold step of shaping his nephew's career path and grooming him personally. In spite of opposition from family and snide comments from people around, he engaged a music teacher and held music lessons for the boy in his own house. Shri Kundan Lal Akhgar, an unsung but promising Urdu poet and author of a few published works, would be a familiar visitor to appreciative homes.

Chapter 6

Lifestyle

It was an inhibited lifestyle with rules set by patriarchs of the family and society at large. Deviations were not tolerated. Good girls oiled their hair into tight braids and covered their head with a '*dupatta*'or veil. Married women completely covered their faces when they ventured out into the market and always chaperoned by a male member of the family. To avoid embarrassment to the women of the house, it was customary for the patriarch of the family to cough or clear his throat aloud to announce his arrival and give them enough time to cover their heads with a dupatta (veil). Social interaction with the opposite sex was taboo and drew the ire of elders. Women dressed conservatively and never sang or danced in public. Words like '*yaar*' or '*dildaar*' were never uttered by respectable girls. A young girl, caught combing her hair outside her house, was once severely reprimanded and driven indoors with the lash of a cane by an elder.

(Centre): Smt. Jamna Devi Kalra (former Head Mistress, Arya Kanya Pathshalla DI Khan flanked by (Left): former student, Smt.Vimla Sachdeva and (Right): daughter-in-law, Smt.Prakash Kalra

Derewal Hindu girls were educated till class 10 at the local Arya Kanya Pathshalla where the medium of instruction was Hindi. Boys went to VB High School, Khalsa School or Mission School where the medium of instruction was English, Urdu or Gurumukhi. For higher studies it was a norm to send boys to Lahore, the centre of learning. According to the Census of India[6],1911 vol.13, literacy among males in Dera Ismail Khan was high and literacy in English was highest among people belonging to the *Brahmin, Arora* and *Khatri* castes. Literacy in English among females was almost absent. According to the census report literacy figures per mile in Dera Ismail Khan, there were 442 Hindu educated males as against 44 Hindu females. Post matriculation, girls could do F.A. at a local college or wait to get married. Arranged marriages within the family fold were a norm and never questioned. Though a male child was preferred as the first-born and thereafter, a girl child was well protected and poured much affection on.

Smt. Ghanshyam Devi, Deputy Head Mistress at Arya Kanya Pathshalla

In an area where women's education was not paid much heed to, Ghanshyam Devi ji did Visharad in Sanskrit (equivalent of Bachelor of Arts) and F.A. (Fellow of Arts) in English. She was offered the post of headmistress at Arya Kanya Pathshalla which she declined and preferred taking on the role of deputy headmistress. Post partition she taught Sanskrit at Birla Arya Girls Senior Secondary School in Kamla Nagar, Delhi, devoting herself to education of girls till her retirement. Her younger sister, Smt Sham Devi Sachdeva, topped in Sanskrit in the Prayag examination in the North-West Frontier Province.

WEDDING TRADITIONS

Derewal Wedding: Elders present (LtoR) Shri Sant Ram Sethi, Smt. Sham Devi Sachdeva, mother of the bridegroom, Subhash Chander and Dr.Lachchman Das Sachdeva.

Wedding procession was called '*janj*' and the ceremony called '*kaaj*'. At the wedding venue the groom's family was welcomed with a recitation of a long verse or '*Sehra*' in praise of the families of the bride and groom. The groom's brother-in-law (sister's husband) was his best-man or '*Aanhar*'. The *Aanhar* carried a sword and was present with the groom throughout the wedding proceedings. The sword symbolised protection of the groom from any negative forces. The wedding trousseau was exhibited in a room for guests to view. A day prior to the wedding, women of the family would dip a finger into red tinted castor oil and apply to the bride's hair. An essential part of a woman's '*shringar* box' (vanity box) was the '*surma*' or kohl powder to darken and beautify the eyes. The '*surmedani*' or container was exquisitely crafted and ideally made of silver. It was applied to the eyes with a smooth silver stick or '*surumchu*'. A set of red and white bangles or '*choodha*' were gifted to the bride by her maternal uncle to be worn on the wedding day. At the *Doli* ceremony (farewell of the bride) a pouch of dry fruits accompanied the bride to her new home signifying prosperity. Departing from her mother's house after the wedding ceremony, the bride would utter the words,

तैडा घर तैडे नाल,
मैडा घर मैडे नाल।

Taida ghar taidey naal,
Maida ghar maidey naal.

Transl.

(Your house will be yours,
My house will be mine.)

Weddings were a month-long celebration with extended families coming together, assisting in arrangements, feasting and uplifting the joyous atmosphere. On the wedding day, as the bridegroom mounted the horse, women of the family would break into song,

साडा गुड़ दा रोड़ा तरिया
इयो परनींदा भागेभरिया
परनींदा तूँ सावरे घर वे
घिन वंझड़ीं घर आ मैडा लाला।

Saada gurh da rorha tarya
Iyo parneenda bhagey bhareya
Parneenda tun sawarey vanj vey
Ghin vanjharhi ghar aa meda lala.

Transl.

(Our sweet-ball of jaggery rejoices at his good fortune of getting married.

My son, go to your bride's parental home and bring back your bride.)

Another folk song sung during weddings goes as below,

हरिया तां भागेभरिया हे
जिस दिहाड़े मैडा हरिया जो जमिया
सोई दिहाड़ा भागे भरिया हे
ते पुछदी पुछदी मालन नगराँ तों आई
शादी वाला घर केड़ा हे?
उची उची माड़ि ते सब्ज़ कनाथां
शादी वाला घर ईयो हे
डू लख चम्बा, त्रै लख मरुआ
पंज लख सेरे दा मुल हे

Bridegroom's mother:

पंज लख डेंदि नी मैं छीं लख डेसां
सेरा तां जड़त जड़ेसां वे
सेरा तां मुंडू ना वलेसाँ मैं

Hariya taan bhaage bharia hey
(Hariya is very fortunate)

Jis dihaade meyda hariya jo jamiya
(The very day my Hariya was born)

Soi dihaada bhaage bharia hey
(That day was very auspicious)

Tey puchhdi puchhdi maalan nagaraan toh aayi
(The gardener's wife has come, all the way from the city, inquiring)

Shaadi vala ghar keda hey?
(In which house is the wedding to be celebrated?)

Uchi uchi maadi tey sabz kanaathaan
(The tall house with green coloured tents)

Shaadi vala ghar iyo hey
(This is the wedding venue)

Du lakh chamba, trai lakh marua
(Two lakh for champa flowers, three lakh for jasmines)

Panj lakh seyrey da mul hey
(Total cost of the floral crown is Rs.5 lakhs)

Bridegroom's mother:

Panj lakh dendhi ni mey chheen lakh deysa
(I will not give five lakhs but six lakh rupees)

Seyra taan jadat jadesaan vey
(The floral crown should appear bejewelled)

Seyra taan mundu na valesaan meyn.
(I will never return the sehra to you.)

In the following wedding song the bridegroom's sister sings,

किथाँ सुखाँवाँ तैडे कपड़े
वे पेके मावाँ नाल
किथाँ सुखाँवाँ रुमाल
राज भिरावाँ नाल
हिक्को डेडियाँ नाल
रल खेडियाँ नाल।

Kithaan sukhavaan taide kapde
(Where can I dry your clothes?)

Ve peke mavaan naal
(Your place is in your parental home)

Kithaan sukhavaan rumaal
(Where can I dry your handkerchief?)

Raj bhiravaan naal
(Your home is with your brothers.)

Hikko dediyaan naal
(Live united together)

Ral khediyaan naal.
(Live together in harmony.)

The day after the wedding, the ritual of 'Til Vetre' was held after which the bride would lift her veil and receive gifts in cash. A pouch filled with black sesame seeds and salt would be exchanged between a woman relative and the bride two to three times. The words, *"Til Vetre, Til Vetre, Sass-Nu de Til Vetre"*, were recited when the mother-in-law conducted the ritual. When the groom's sister would do so the words changed to, *"Til Vetre, Til Vetre, Ninarh-Bharjai de Til Vetre"*. Black sesame seeds had a special significance in this ritual as it was believed to dispel negativity. The verse recited by the mother-in-law goes as below:

तिल वेत्रे तिल वेत्रे
सस्स नू दे तिल वेत्रे
डेवाँ मै, घिने तूँ
ख़ुशियाँ डेसें, पुतर जमेसें।

Transl. (*Til Vetre, Til Vetre,*

Til Vetre ritual between mother-in-law and daughter-in-law
I offer, you receive,
Bestow upon us joy, with the birth of a baby boy.)

Chapter 7

Rituals and Folk Lore

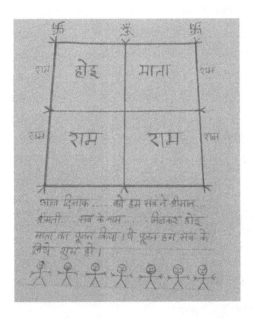

The festival of '*Hoi*' (होई) was celebrated eight days before Diwali. *Mata Hoi* (माता होई), the Goddess and protector of children was worshipped by drawing a square divided into four parts on the wall. The drawing was done with '*geru*' or natural red colour and had religious symbols such as *Om* (ॐ), *Swastika* and *Ram Ram* (राम राम) written. The pandit's wife would come to make the drawing and perform *arti* (prayers) in front of it. The mother would tap the door of the house with a '*belan*' (बेलन) (rolling-pin) and call out,

होई, होई ,होई
दरवाज़े पिच्छे खड़ी होई।

Hoi, Hoi, Hoi
Darwaze pichhey khari Hoi.

Transl. (*Mata Hoi, Hoi, Hoi*

Who stands behind the door.)

Her children, standing behind the door, would open a chink of the door and call out on behalf of the Goddess,

दुध पुतर डित्तेमी
डिवा मैडी डोई।

Dudh putar dittemi
Diva maidi doi.

Transl. (I have given you milk and children, give me my offering.)

The mother would hand over '*prasad*' or offering, through the chink of the door, to the children. This was repeated three times with the mother knocking at the door and the children repeating the Goddess Hoi's request and receiving the offering. The offering was in the form of a thin, bland '*mathi*' (मठी) known as '*Chanderkala*' (deep-fried flour pancake) and '*latee*' (लेटी) or *atta halwa* with a softer consistency than normal *halwa*. Festive sweets distributed on this day were sweet '*tikkare*' (मिठे टिक्कड़े), '*parakarhi*' (पराकड़ी) and '*mathian*' (मठियाँ). '*Parakarhi*' is the Derewali name for '*gujiya*'.

'*Tikka*', a festival symbolising the bond between a brother and sister, is celebrated two days after *Diwali*. As the sister applies '*tikka*' on the brother's forehead, a mark of protection, she recites the following verse,

सूरज डितियाँ लासाँ,
ते चंद्र डित्ता उभार,
ते भींणी-भिरा दा टिकड़ा,
यम परेरे जा।

Suraj dittian laasaan,
Te Chandra ditta ubhaar,
Te bheendi-bhira da tikda,
Yam parere ja.

Transl.

The sun spreads its rays,

The moon has shone its beams,

Tikka, the bond of a sister and brother is so strong that even *Yama*, the God of Death, keeps away.

The festival of *Lohri* (Harvest festival) saw children visiting homes, receiving money and sweets and singing,

लकड़ी डेसें पुतर जमेसें
गोया डेसें धी जमेसें
लोड़ी डेओ, लोड़ी डेओ।

Lakdi deysey putar jameysey
(If you give us firewood a son will be born to you)

Goya deysey dhee jameysey
(If you give us a cow-dung cake a daughter will be born to you)

Lorhi deyo, Lorhi deyo
(Give us offerings, Give us offerings for *Lorhi*.)

The festival of *Poonrhi* was celebrated a day after *Lohri* when young girls would come to bless and sing to a new-born baby boy and receive gifts. The girls would offer small tufts of cotton wool at the feet of the infant as they sang,

पूँड़ी वे काका पूँड़ी, तैडी जोय ते डाढ़ी सूँड़ी,

अधि सूँड़ी ते अधि परूँड़ी,

लोला वे काका लोला,

तैडे मा प्यू दा हिंडोला,

खटन वाला प्यू जीवे

साम्भन वाली मा जीवे

काकड़े दी मा, डू चार फुलड़े चड़ा,

चुँण चुँण झोलियाँ भरा

जीवे प्यू ते भिरा।

काका रोंदा पिया

पैले काके कूँ चा

वत आना डिवा।

Transl.

Poonrhi vey kaka Poornhi
(It is the festival of Poornhi Oh baby boy)

Taidi Joyeh tey dadhi soorhi
(Your wife will be very pretty)

Adhi soorhi tey adhi paroonrhi
(Partly pretty and partly plain)

Lola vey kaka lola
(O sweet baby boy)

Taidey Ma Pyu Da hindola
(The object of your parents' affection)

Khattan vala Pyu jeevey
(Long live your father who fends for you)

Saamban vali Ma jeevey
(Long live your mother who tends to you)

Kaakadey di Ma, du-char phularhey chadaa
(Mother of the baby boy, offer some corn to the fire)

Chun chun jholiyan bhara
(May you be blessed with prosperity)

Jeevey Pyu tey Bhira
(Long live your father and brother)

Kaka ronda piya,
(The baby boy is wailing)

Paile kake kun cha
(First pick up the baby boy)

Vat anna diva.
Then give us an anna.)

Prediction of the gender of the next baby was an interesting pastime. Women regaled themselves by asking the young sibling of an unborn child to choose between a crow or mynah (काँ के लाली) or choose a stick or stone (लकड़ी के वड्डा). If the child chose a crow or stone it meant a male-child. A mynah or stick signified a girl-child. Another guessing game was making the young child stand and observe which foot was raised first. Lifting of the right foot meant a baby boy and lifting the left foot signified a baby girl. They humoured themselves singing:

ओलना-घोलना, सिवा डिवाई चोलना
सज्जा पैर चा तूँ
खब्बे कूँ वत्ता तूँ।

Olna-gholna, sivaa diwaa-een cholna
Sajja Peyr cha tun
Khabbey ku vata tun.

The above verse is obviously favouring the birth of a son as women are promising to stitch new clothes for the child if he/she lifts the right foot.

Song dotingly sung to a kid who was teething:

डंदामनी बकरी, टोपा डेंदी खीर दा,
साडे वेड़े आंदी हे, छिक मराई तीर दा।

Danda Mani bakri, topa deyndi kheer da
(Oh toothless goat who gives milk in a vessel)

Saadey Veyrhey aandi hey chhik maraayee teer da.
(If you come to our backyard we will scare you by shooting arrows)

A mother would sing this rhyme as she rocked her child up and down on her feet:

झूटे माईयाँ, पैर कूँ वधाइयाँ,
पैर गिया दिल्ली
पकड़ घिन आया बिल्ली
बिल्ली डे डू बच्चे
भगवान साँई सच्चे।

Jhutey maiya, peyr ku vadhaiyaan
(Swing, swing. The feet be praised.)

Peyr gaya Dilli, pakarh ghin aya billi
(The feet went to Delhi and brought back a cat.)

Billi dey du bachey
(The cat had two kittens.)

Bhagwan Sain sachey
(God is truthful.)

Leisure hours and play time were fun-filled as girls clapped high-fives and sang the following rhyme,

अम्बे डी माए अम्बे
तैडे सत भिरा मंगे
तैडा हिक भिरा कुँवारा
ओ चोपड़ खेडन आला

ओ चोपड़ किथाँ खेडे
लहोर शैर खेडे
लहोर शैर उच्चा
मै मन्न पकाया सुच्चा
मैडे मन्न कूँ लगे मोती
मै भींड़ कूँ सडवाया
मै सौ रुपैया लाया
मैडा हिक रुपैया खोटा
मै भींड़ कूँ मारा सोटा
अम्बे डी माए अम्बे

Ambe di maaye Ambe
Taide sat bhira mange
Taida hik bhira kunwara
O chopad khedan ala
O chopad kithaan khede
Lahore shair khede
Lahore shair uchcha
Mai mann pakaya suchcha
Maide mann kun lagge moti
Mai bheend kun sadvaya
Mai sau rupaiya laya
Maida hik rupaiya khota
Mai bheend kun maara sota
Ambe di maaye Ambe.

Transl.

(This verse is addressed to a girl named, Ambe.)

Your seven brothers are betrothed

Except for one, who remains single,

The one who spends time playing 'chopad'

Where does he play the game?

He plays in the big city of Lahore.

I have hygienically cooked 'mann' (thick corn roti)

My 'mann' should be relished as it has been cooked with love.

I invited my sister for a lavish meal that cost me Rs.100/-

She gave me a fake rupee coin for which I beat her with a stick.)

Lullaby

लो....लो....लो....लो आँ लोरी डेवाँ
लोरी डेवाँ निक्के बाल कूँ
आ वे रामजी आ तूँ
निक्केयाँ बालाँ कूँ खिडा तूँ
साडी गल्ली रामजी आया
बालाँ ने सुख पाया
रामजी ने बालाँ कूँ गोद विच खिडाया।
आ वे रामजी आ तूँ।

Lo....lo....lo....lo aa lori devaan
Lori devaan nikke baal kun
Aa vey Ramji aa tun
Nikeyaan baalaan kun khida tun
Saadi galli Ramji aya
Baalaan ne sukh paya
Ramji ne baalaan kun godh vich khidaya
Aa vey Ramji aa tun.

Transl.

(Sound made by rolling the tongue in the mouth.

Come let me sing a lullaby to a small child.

Come Lord Rama, come and play with small children.

Lord Rama has come to our street.

The children are pacified as Rama plays with them on his lap.)

Children were taught moral values and piety in the following verse,

वाहेगुरू वाहेगुरू आख
तैडा खंड भरीजे वात
वाहेगुरू वाहेगुरू बोल
तैडा के लगसी मोल।

Waheguru Waheguru aakh,
Taida khand bharije waat,
Waheguru Waheguru bol,
Taida ke lagsi mol.

Transl.

(Utter the name of God

Your mouth will be filled with sweetness.

Utter the name of God,

It will cost you nothing.)

Chicken-pox and small-pox were deadly diseases for which the Goddess '*Daati*' was propitiated. When a child was afflicted with pox it meant the goddess (*Mata*) '*Daati*' had visited the house and a song in her praise was sung to the sick child,

मैं आई खड़ियाँ, कुछढ़ पाई खड़ियाँ,
डाती डे बिखिया मैं घर चल्लियां
डे बिखिया मैं घर चल्लियां
डाती डे बिखिया मैं घर चल्लियां।
ओ मैडी डाती दा अज बखीयार
सो ख़यालां वाली दा धवां डे नन्धड़ा बाल
वण डाती कौण तैडी बुहारी डेवे
वण मैया कौण तैडी बुहारी डेवे
कौण करे छिंणकार

ओ मैडी डाती दा अज बखियार
सो ख़यालां वाली दा धवां डे नन्धड़ा बाल।

Mey aayi kharhian, kuchharh paayi kharhian
(I am standing with a child in my arms)

Daati dey bhikhiya mey ghar chaliyan
(Mata Daati bestow your blessings as I return home)

Repeat:

Dey bhikhiya mey ghar chaliyan
Daati dey bhikhiya mey ghar chaliyan
O meydi Daati da ajj bakhiyar
(Today is your celebration, my goddess)

So khayalan wali da dhavadey nandharha baal
(You, who is all-knowing, please bathe (purify) my child)

Varhn Daati, kaun teydi buhari deyvey
(Dear Daati, who will sweep the place for you)

Varhn Maiyya, kaun teydi buhari deyvey
Kaun karey chhirhnkar
(Who will sprinkle water)

O meydi Daati da ajj bakhiyar
(Today is your celebration, my goddess)

So khayala wali da dhavadey nandharha baal
(You, who is all-knowing, please bathe (purify) my child)

In the following song Sant Kabir admonishes his wife Lohi for cheapening the name of Lord Rama. She had advised a visiting leper to chant Lord Rama's name three times to cure his disease when chanting only once was enough for his prayers to be answered.

लोईए राम दी पियारिए,
तैं राम कूँ सस्ता लाया
त्रै वारी राम अखाके
कोढ़ी दा कोढ़ मिटाया।

Transl.

Lohiye Ram di Piyariye
(Lohi, devotee of Lord Rama)

Teyn Ram ku sasta laya
(You have cheapened the name of Lord Rama)

Trey vari Ram akha ke
(By repeating 'Ram' three times)

Korhi da Korh mitaya
(To cure the leper of leprosy.)

A bearded mendicant, with bloodshot eyes which would scare the life of little children, would frequent the door-step of homes for alms with his refrain:

वस्से राणी जीवें पुतर ते वडा थीवे
वंज के माँ दे कोलूं होवे
के बेड़ी निकल वैसी
बिलोटो यारो।

Vassey Rani, jeevey putar tey vadda theevey
Vanj ke ma de kol hovey
Ke beydi nikal veysi
Biloto yaaro.

Transl.

(May your daughter flourish, may your son grow up to live long

And go soon to stay with his mother

Or else he will miss the boat to Bilot, friends.)

The plaintive verse of a wounded and dying female rat is addressed to a Brahmin (priest) who is bathing at a well nearby:

धाता-धूता बामण
इस्नान करेंदा बामण
वंज आखें मैडी भिंनण कूँ
जो रा खटेन्दी मोई मोई
अज के, कल के, कल के क़ल्लथूँ।

Dhata dhuta baamarhn
Isnaan karenda baamarhn
Vanj aakhen meydi bhinnarhn ku
Jo raah khatendi moi moi
Aj ke, kal ke, kal ke, kallathun

Transl.

(Oh Brahmin who bathes

Go tell my sister who is waiting for me

That I am dying

Today, tomorrow or the day-after.)

Another song sung by my paternal grandmother:

पुढी बुहारी कैं डित्ती ओए?
पुढी बुहारी कैं डित्ती ओए?
ते किस बूए सट्टी सुआ ओए जी?
असां पन्धेणऊ पाँधणए, ते तूँ खीसे विच दुआ ओए जी
हँजू ना ठुल्का ओए जी।

Transl.

Putthi buhaari keyn diti oiye
Putthi buhaari keyn diti oiye
(Who has swept the ground the wrong way?)

Tey kis booyeh suttee sua oiye ji?
(And in front of whose door has the fire-ash been thrown?)

Assaan panderhu paanderhey, tey tun kheesey vich dua oiye ji
(We are travellers walking barefoot, so fill our pocket with your prayers)

Hanju na thulka oiye ji
(Do not shed tears)

Raja Rasalu was a legendary king. His mother pined for him when he left home and expressed her desire to have him back. In this verse, she addresses the vazir or minister's pet parrot and mynah to go and persuade the Raja to return home,

तोता ओए वज़ीर दा
मैना ओए वज़ीर दी,
तूँ राजे कूँ वला घिन आ
जे तूँ भुक्खा धन दा
ते उड्ड डेसाँई लधवा ओएजी
जे तूँ भुक्खा रनां दा
तां लख डेसाई परना ओएजी।

Transl.

Tota oiye vazir da, myna oiye vazir di
(Oh parrot and mynah belonging to the minister,)

Tu raje ku vala ghinna
(Please go and persuade the Raja to return home)

Tell him,

Jey tun bhukkha dhan da
(If you hunger for wealth)

Tey utth deysaayin ladhva oiye ji
(Then I will give you a camel-load full of riches.)

Jey tun bhukkha runna da
(If you lust for women)

Taan lakh deysaayin parnaa oiye ji
(Then I will get you married a lakh times) *hundred thousand

A verse recited by kids:

निक्की जीं सीटी
वंज पई मसीटी
मुल्ला धाड़ धाड़ कीती।

"*Nikki ji seety*
Vanj payi maseeti
Mulla dhaarh dhaarh keeti"

Transl.

(A tiny ant enters the mosque to the annoyance of the Mullah.)

A sad verse about a thirsty Persian boy who died asking for water because nobody understood the language he spoke:

आभ आभ करेंदा मोया बचड़ा
फ़ारसियाँ दे घर तूँ
अगर मैं जाँडदी तूँ मंगदा पाणी
मैं डेंदि भर भर प्याले।

Transl.

Aabh Aabh karenda moya bachrha
(A child died crying, "water, water")

Farsiyaan dey ghar tun
(From a Persian home)

Agar meyn jaarhndi tun mangda pani
(Had I known you wanted water)

Meyn dendi bhar bhar pyalley.
(I would have given many cups full.)

At dusk it was customary for women to switch on lights or light a lamp and sing in praise of Goddess, Mata Tarni, with hands folded in prayer. Mata Tarni was beseeched to assuage all sufferings of humanity. Four parts of the day are spent doing personal chores but to spare just one moment to remember God is enough. Sparing even half a moment is enough for us to attain salvation and receive God's grace.

तार माता तारनी,
सब दुःख निवारनी,
चार पहर घर दा काम,
हिक घड़ी ले हर दा नाम,
हिक घड़ी ना अद घड़ी,
अद घड़ी परवान हे
राम जी मेहरबान हे
तार माता तारनी।

Taar Mata Taarni,
Sab dukh nivarni,
Char pahar ghar da kaam,
Hik ghari ley Har da naam,
Hik ghari na adh ghari
Adh ghari parvaan hey
Ram ji meharbaan hey
Taar mata Taarni.

Chapter 8

Bohriyan Wala Thalla

(Sacred pilgrimage shrine)[7]

Pilgrims from far off places thronged to Bilot, located 35 miles north of D I Khan, between the river Indus and the mountain range of Sheikh Budin. At a peaceful spot, under the shade of a peepal tree was *Bohriyan Wala Thalla* or '*samadhi*' where the 17th century saint, Gossain Sati Kewal Ramji sat in meditation. At his shrine devotees would congregate to pray for favours, seek the saint's blessings and listen to his discourses. A verse, in praise of the saint, begins with the lines[8],

"Jai hovi bohriyan wala
Taidi kudrat tun meherbaan."

It was customary for Hindus to perform '*jhand*' (tonsure), '*chola*' (clothes for the newborn), and '*janeyu*' ceremonies at the shrine. The shrine drew crowds throughout the year especially during the festival of Baisakhi when a fair was organised. '*Prasad*' or offering distributed to the worshippers was in the form of '*mishri*' or sugar candy. Nearby was the shrine of a pious Muslim '*pir*' (sage) whose name was Sheikh Issa Kataar Sahib. He, too, was impressed by the miraculous blessings of Gossain Kewal Ramji and visited his shrine. Soon Muslim pilgrims, flocked in large numbers. He was known as '*Sati*' Kewal Ramji Bohriyan Wala as he was a seeker of the ultimate truth and led a selfless and austere life. Sati Kewal Ramji was the grandson of Gossain Lalji Maharaj who was known to have bestowed miraculous blessings upon his devotees who sought his help. Though there is no historical evidence, it has been told that as his disciples grew in numbers he found it difficult to concentrate on his meditation and suddenly disappeared from Bilot. He is known to have reached Sindh to seek solace in the jungle. He came to be known as 'Lal Shahbaaz' among his Muslim devotees. In that spot there is a 'dargah' (tomb) where devotees offer prayers.

Chapter 9

Language

'Saraiki' is a post-partition nomenclature for languages which are similar such as Derewali, Multani, Lahnda, Jatki, Sindhi, Bahawalpuri and are spoken with slight variations depending upon the region. According to historians Saraiki is an ancient language and is categorized under the Indo-Aryan group of languages. It is believed that prior to the Muslim invasions, a dialect of Prakrit was spoken in the Indus Valley. The *Rig Veda* is believed to be composed in this region in the vicinity of Multan.

Derewali, the language of my parents, was a spoken language without a script of its own. Women folk would converse with each other in Derewali but letter writing was done in Hindi using the Devanagri script. Men folk would converse in Derewali but letter writing was done in Urdu or English. In this respect Derewali was rarely written in the Devanagri script. After the partition very few parents encouraged their children to speak the language. Perhaps, in their view, it was no longer relevant with the change of scene.

In his book[9], 'The Seraiki Language', M Bashir Ahmad Zami Bahawalpuri, the author, states,"......no power can oust a language unless the people who speak it are driven away from that country and this is physically impossible." These words seem so ironic in the case of the Hindu Derewals as history proved the author wrong. History witnessed an unprecedented exodus from the soil of their ancestors.

Derewali has a unique identity and is regarded as different from Punjabi. The region where the Saraiki language is spoken, had been ravaged by several invading armies and, over centuries, had absorbed the language and culture of its invaders. Besides some similarities due to proximity with the Punjab, there is a marked disparity in culture and language of the two regions. Clear differences between the two languages are listed below:

Derewali	English	Punjabi
Ghin (घिन्न)	Take	Leh (लै)
Ghattaan (घत्तां)	Put	Pavaan (पावाँ)
Kaaj (काज)	Wedding	Vya (व्या)
Trimath (त्रिमत)	Woman	Zanani (ज़नानी)
Chhor (छोर)	Boy	Munda (मुंडा)
Chhvayr (छवेर)	Girl	Kurhi (कुड़ी)
Bhannya (भन्नया)	Broken	Tutya (टुट्या)
Kheesa (खीसा)	Pocket	Jeyb (जेब)
Kuvaar (कुवार)	Wife	Voti (वोटी)
Bheenrh (भींण)	Sister	Panrh (पैंण)
Bhiraa (भिरा)	Brother	Pra (प्रा)
Vassal (वस्सल)	Onion	Pyaz (प्याज़)
Kheer (खीर)	Milk	Dudh (दुध)
Vaysoon (वैसूँ)	will go	Jawangey (जावाँगे)
Khileya (खिल्लेया)	Laughed	Hassya (हस्स्या)
Saaku (साकु)	to us	Saanu (सानूँ)
Unaaku (उन्नाकु)	to them	Unaanu (उनानू)
Assaan (अस्साँ)	Us	Assee (अस्सी)
Tussaan (तुस्साँ)	You	Tussee (तुस्सी)
Baal (बाल)	Child	Bachha (बच्चा)

Ithaan (इथाँ)	Here	Ithay (इथे)
Uthaan (उथाँ)	There	Uthay (उथे)
Hik (हिक)	One	Ik (इक)
Du (डू)	Two	Do (दो)
Treh (त्रै)	Three	Tin (तिन)
Chheen (छीं)	Six	Chhay (छे)
Da (डा)	Ten	Dus (दस)

Wit and sarcasm surface in day to day Derewali conversation. Some delightful witticisms, sayings and expressions are listed below:

Q. त्वाडा के हाल हे?

Twada kay haal hay?
Transl. (How are you?)

A. सिर गिची दे नाल हे।

Sir gichi day naal hay.
Transl. (My head is lodged on my neck.)

बुख लगी ताँ भूसा खा
त्रै लगी ताँ खू ख़टवा
थक गयी तां मैकू चा।

Bukh lagi taan bhoosa kha
Transl. (If you are hungry, eat wheat straw.)

Tray lagi taan khu khatva
Transl. (If you are thirsty, dig a well.)

Thukk gayin taan makku cha.
Transl. (If you are tired, carry me.)

ना मूँह ना मथा
ते जिन्न पहाड़ूँ लथा

Na mu na matha
Tay jinn paharhu laththa

Transl. (One who appears unimpressive but puts on a superior attitude.)

आखाँ धी कूँ, सुणावाँ नू कूँ।
Aakhaan dhi ku, surhaavaan nu ku

Transl. (Complaints addressed to the daughter but intended for the daughter-in-law who is within hearing distance.)

रज खादे दी मार।
Rujj khaaday di maar

Transl. (Even if there is excess food, you are not satiated and still have cravings.)

फुल ना डेंदी माँगवाँ
गैइए बाग लुटा।

Phul na dayndi maangvaan
Gaiyay baag lutaa

Transl. (In your life-time you do not give a single flower to anyone, but after you die, your garden is neglected and in ruins.)

गो कु मिले गो
जीयाँ ओ ते जीयाँ ओ।

Go ku milay go
Jeeyaan oh te jeeyaan oh

Transl. (Meeting of two lazy persons who have so much in common between them.)

मावाँ धीयाँ आपो आप
बुआ भतीजी हिक्का ज़ात।

Maanvaan dheeyaan aapo aap
Bua bhateeji hikka zaat.

Transl. (Mother and daughter bond naturally but a paternal aunt and niece have family ties.)

आपणे जाये नित
ते मा प्यू जाये कित।

Aaprhey jaaye nith
Tay ma pyu jaaye kith.

Transl. (Your own children will be close to you but your siblings or offsprings of your mother and father will drift apart.)

मोहन दे लारे परनींदे वी कुआरें।
Mohan de laare parneende vi kuware.

Transl. (A person who commits to doing a job but never does it is akin to a married man who remains a bachelor.)

ना कम दा ना कार दा।
Na kam da na kar da

Transl. (Good for nothing person.)

ज़ाल, बाल, मुछ दा वाल
रख सम्भाल।

Zaal baal muchh da vaal
Rakh sambhaal

Transl. (Your wife, your children and your moustache are to be kept safe.)

A hungry, wailing baby was affectionately called, 'Bukkha Bangali' (hungry Bengali), alluding to the great famine in Bengal.

छज्जु जो सुख चबारे
ओ बलख़ ना बुख़ारे।

Chhajju jo sukh chabaare
O Balakh na Bukhare.

Transl. (Women would advise their husbands not to leave home for another town. The comfort you get in your own home will not be there even if you travel to Balkh or Bukhara in Afghanistan.)

ईवेंई घुंगलुआँ तूँ मिट्टी उतरेंदा पै।

Transl. (A person who speaks superficially, without meaning what he says. Literal meaning is to remove mud from turnips.)

घर दा जोगी जोगड़ा बाहर दा जोगी सिद्ध।

Transl. (A person who is taken for granted at home but is highly respected outside.)

उत्तूँ दी मैं चखी मक्खी
अंदरूँ दी मैं बुड़ बुड़ त्रकी।

Transl. (A person who flaunts a cosmetic exterior but is unhygienic and filthy inside. Metaphorically it could mean deceiving others with an impressive demeanour but being vile and vicious inside.)

मै ताँ बन्दे कूँ खा गई हे।
Meyn taan bande kun kha gai hey.

Transl. (His ego is consuming him)

आगा दौड़ ते पीछा छोड़।
Aaga daudh te peechha chhod.

Transl. (Often elders would chide someone for ignoring life's learnings from the past in search of novel experiences.)

ज्जाए सिखेन्दे आए।

Jaye sikhende aaye.

Transl. (A sarcastic comment by an elderly person about how the younger generation is trying to teach them.)

दिल्ली शैर नमूना
अंदर मिट्टी बाहर चूना।

Dilli shair namoona
Andar mitti bahar choona.

Transl. (Perception of Delhi is different from reality. Refugees who were in great distress and disillusioned with their new home town, would often express that Delhi had a white-washed exterior but mud inside.)

उड़सी कुर्सी
कंध एरे ते टुर्सी।

Udsi kursi
Kandh erey te tursi .

Transl. (Just as a high wall is built on a strong foundation, a person can elevate himself only on the basis of his early upbringing and values.)

भिरा भिरावाँ दे,
ते चिचड़ कावाँ दे।

Bhira bhiravaan dey
Te chichad kavaan dey.

Transl. (Brothers are to brothers

As ticks are to crows.) This expression is used to describe the strong bond between brothers.

हाए मैडे रब्बा
तूँ डे दुनिया दा डब्बा

Hai mede rabba,
Tun de duniya da dabba.

Transl. (Oh my God, bestow the world's wealth upon me.)

साग रोटी पछा ताईं
खिचड़ी डूपारा ताईं
साईं मोअन भत्त डे जो चौके दी बनाली ताईं।

Transl. (A diet of *saag* and *roti* can sustain us till the evening. *Khichadi* can barely sustain us till the afternoon but a meal of rice or *bhaat* is so light that just as one walks out along the *naali* or kitchen water drainage channel one feels hunger pangs.)

पंडितजी जमदे क्यो ना मोए।
पैले ताँ खान्दे हावे डुध-मलाईयाँ,
अजकल खान्दे वे सुक्के गोए।

The above verse reflects the scarcities that prevailed at some point in time that affected the flow of offerings to the priests.

Transl. Panditji was it not better to die than be born to suffer the fate that has befallen you. You saw days of plenty when you could have a diet of milk and cream. Today you have nothing but dry cow dung cakes.

बाल: माई नी माई मासी आई।
माँ: फ़िट गधेयाँ दी टासी आई।
बाल: माई नी माई सिर ते पंड सू।
माँ: हरदम आवे, नित नित आवे,
जदंण तक भींण दा दम सू।

The above conversation is a reflection of hypocrisy of a woman towards her own sister who is unwelcome in her house. The moment she knows her sister is carrying gifts for her, she welcomes her whole-heartedly proclaiming her doors are open till she is alive.

Blessings in Derewali:

वडा वडा बख्त लगेई।

May you get good fortune.

बख्ताँ आला।

Fortunate person.

बचड़े जीवणी।

May your children live. (This expression was often used as child mortality was prevalent.)

Chapter 10

Food Traditions

During the British rule, Hindu and Muslim communities lived in separate areas. Hindus were mostly vegetarians and their cuisine was distinctive of their habitat. They had living legends like Gela halwai and Pokhar halwai who were known for their delicious *'purnis'* (*kachoris*), *pakoras* and *bhor* (fried batter remnants of *pakora*) and mouth-watering *'Sone Halwa'*. *Sone Halwa* is available in Delhi by the name of 'dhodha burfi'. It is traditionally cooked with *'soni'* or *'angoori'*, an important ingredient in the making of the halwa. The sprouts which emerge from germinated wheat, are dried in shade and then pounded. This dried ingredient (*angoori*) when mixed in milk curdles and gives the halwa its grainy texture. The origin of Sone Halwa is not clear but some trace it to the Persians in the 16th century when the Mughal Emperor Humayun came back to power after being exiled in Herat. Some claim it was introduced by Diwan Sawan Mal, the ruler of Multan in 1750. Another story goes that a king's daughter saw a Hindu vendor selling this halwa and was so delighted by the taste that she named it *Sone Halwa*. Home-made delicacies were *'Lolley'* or balls made of sweetened wheat dough deep-fried. *'Doli di Roti'* or fermented wheat *roti* (bread) was made by kneading wheat flour with boiling hot water, *khus khus* (poppy seeds), gram dal flour, cinnamon, cloves and jaggery. *'Jeera'* was a sweet prepared in winter using jaggery, *jeera* and *somf*, cut into square pieces and given to nursing mothers. It was customary to offer a small *roti* to the fire before beginning to cook a meal. This practice was called *'Visarhn'*.

A typical Derewal cuisine had dishes such as *'teetak da bartha'*. *Teetak* is a wild vegetable which looks like a baby water melon. A bitter tasting dish is made from an edible cactus known as *'Choonga'*. *'Peepun'* or a sour parasitic growth from the roots of a *Peelu* tree, was used for making pickle. Another dish savoured by Derewals was *'Chibarh'* or small size parwals (pointed gourd). *'Swanjniyaan de phul'* or the drumstick tree flowers, were cooked into a savoury dish. Another favourite was *'Bhey de pakorey'* (Lotus-stem coated with gram-flour batter and deep-fried). *'Aadey Baadey da Achar'*, a pickle named after its shop owner, *'Aada Baada'*, was very popular. On festive occasions, a special treat *'Zarda'* (Sweet saffron coloured rice loaded with raisins and nuts) was prepared. *Phirni* and *Kheer* are two rice and milk based desserts. *Phirni* is made of powdered rice and milk and set like custard whereas *Kheer* is cooked with whole rice and milk to a thick consistency. *Kheerni* is a dessert with a slight variation as the ingredient used is vermicelli and milk. These desserts are garnished with saffron, cardamom powder, almonds and pistachios.

Winters saw an abundance of vegetables to be consumed, pickled and dried in preparation for the lean months of summer. Women of the house strung garlands of cubed turnips and florets of cauliflower with a needle and thread and hung them in the sun to dry till they shrivelled and dehydrated. These were stored away from moisture and cooked when vegetables were scarce.

Some culinary traditions have been preserved and handed down since generations. A few original recipes are documented below.

RECIPES

LADOOS (लड्डू)

(These were prepared for pregnant women.) *This is an old family recipe courtesy Rita Sethi, handed down from her mother, Late Vidya Sachdeva.*

Ingredients:

1 kg Atta (Whole wheat flour)
1 kg Sugar (powdered)
1 kg pure ghee
200 gms Phool Makhana (Fox nuts)
1 small dry Coconut
250 gms Gond
50 gms Melon seeds
250 gms Almonds
Small quantities of Walnuts, Raisins and Cashewnuts
10 gms white pepper
20 gms Ajwain (Carom seeds)

Method:

1. Roast 1 kg Atta in 1 kg ghee till light golden brown.
2. Grind phool makhana.
3. Grind gond.
4. Coarsely grind all dry fruits.
5. Grate dry coconut.
6. While roasting atta, add ground gond and roast with atta till fluffy.
7. Then add phool makhana and all dry ingredients. Mix well and continue roasting.
8. Now add grated dry coconut.
9. Mix well on low flame.
10. Switch off flame and let the mixture cool for some time and then add sugar.
11. Mix well and make balls when the mixture is luke-warm.

SAAG (साग)

(This dish was specially prepared to feed Pandits during 'Sharad' puja). *Recipe is courtesy Rita Sethi who has shared it from her maternal grand-mother, Late Shanti Devi's family kitchen.*)

Ingredients:

500 gms (approx.) Palak (spinach leaves)
250 gms Arbi
100-150 gms Bhindi (lady's finger)
1 large brinjal
150 gms Loki (bottle gourd)
2 potatoes
2-3 green chillies
3-4 tomatoes

Method:

1. Finely chop the spinach.
2. Chop all vegetables except potatoes into small pieces.
3. Wash and put spinach and chopped vegetables into a cooker.
4. Cook on low flame till fully cooked.
5. Mash them well but do not blend in the mixie.
6. Cut potatoes into small cubes, fry them and keep aside.
7. Take 2-3 tablespoons of pure ghee for tarka (seasoning).
8. Heat ghee in a pan. When hot, add garam masala and dry coriander powder. Add the mashed spinach mixture.
9. Add fried potatoes. Keep stirring till the water evaporates and oil is released.
10. Saag is ready to serve.

PURNI (पूरनी)

(This was a popular snack also known as kachori. *Recipe courtesy Vimla Sachdeva*)

Ingredients:

2 cups Maida (refined flour)
1 cup Atta (whole wheat flour)
Pinch of Salt
¼ cup oil

1 ½ cup Mung dhuli dal
Warm water for kneading
4-5 whole pepper corns
1 tsp jeera (cumin seeds)
¼ tsp Ajwain (carom seeds)
1 tblp Besan (gram flour)
½ tsp garam masala
Mint leaves-few
Coriander chopped
Salt to taste
Oil for frying.

Method:

Knead maida, atta, pinch of salt with ¼ cup oil and warm water. Dough should not be very soft.

For Peethi filling:

1. Soak 1 ½ cup of mung dal in water for 10-15 minutes.
2. Boil dal in a little water with salt to taste and 4-5 pepper-corns. When half-cooked, add 1 tsp. oil, jeera, 1 tblsp besan, ajwain, garam masala, fresh mint leaves and fresh coriander and stir.
3. Take off from fire and drain any extra water.
4. When cool flatten balls of kneaded dough and fill with peethi and seal the purnis.
5. Heat the oil on high flame. Thereafter reduce to medium flame and deep fry purnis till light golden brown and crisp.

LOLLEY (लोल्ले)

(Deep fried sweet whole-wheat balls prepared as part of Lohri festivities during harvest-time.)

Recipe courtesy Kamal Grover.

Ingredients:

2 cups Atta (whole-wheat flour)

2-3 tblsp Refined oil

½ tsp Somf (fennel seeds)

1 medium size ball of jaggery

1 tblsp sugar

Oil for frying.

Method:

1. Melt jaggery and sugar in a little hot water.
2. Strain the liquid to clear it.
3. Mix the sweet liquid into atta, add fennel seeds and refined oil.
4. Knead the mixture into a dough of not so soft consistency.
5. Shape into small balls.
6. Deep fry on medium flame till golden brown.

SWANJHNIYA DI SABZI (स्वांझणियाँ दी सब्ज़ी)

(*Traditional dish shared by Kamal Grover*. This dish is made from the buds of the drum-stick tree)

Ingredients:

100 gms buds of Swanjhniya.

1 tblsp pure ghee

Tiny piece Hing (asafoetida)

Small onion finely chopped

½ cup curd (yogurt)

½ cup water

¼ tsp Haldi powder (turmeric)

½ tsp jeera (cumin seeds)

½ tsp dhania powder (coriander)

1 green chilly

Salt as per taste.

Method:

1. Wash the swanjhniya buds well and boil in a pan with 1 glassful of water to which a little salt has been added.
2. When soft strain and wash the swanjhniyan well. Squeeze out the bitterness from the buds.
3. In a pan heat 1 tblsp of pure ghee and fry the chopped onion.
4. Add hing, jeera, dhania powder, green chilly, haldi, and salt to taste.
5. Stir and add the boiled swanjhniya buds. Saute well with the spices.
6. Add ½ cup curd and ½ cup water. Stir till thick and ghee releases from the side.

CHOORI (चूरी)

(Traditional dish prepared during Janamashtami along with gurh-jeera. Choori and gurh jeera was also distributed to friends to celebrate the birth of a child.) *Recipe courtesy Kamal Grover.*

Ingredients:

2 cups Atta (whole-wheat flour)
½ cup refined oil
½ cup sugar (or as per taste) lightly ground in mixie
2½ tblsp pure ghee

Method:

1. Mix atta and refined oil along with a little water and knead to form a hard dough.
2. Divide the dough into three parts and form balls.
3. Make a ½ inch thick roti with a belna (rolling pin) and cook on low flame on a tawa (heavy bottom pan) without any oil.
4. Slow cook on both sides till golden brown.
5. Take off from heat and let the rotis cool.
6. Break the roti into pieces and grind in the mixie to form a powder.

7. In a pan heat 2 ½ tblsps pure ghee. Add the choori powder. Stir and heat very well.

8. Switch off the flame and then add ½ cup sugar (or as per taste) and serve.

GURH JEERA (गुढ़ जीरा)

(Besides being a festive dish, gurh jeera was beneficial for nursing mothers.)

Courtesy Kamal Grover

Ingredients:

1 ½ tblsp Jeera
100 gms jaggery
1 tblsp pure ghee

Method:

1. In a pan roast jeera partially and keep aside.
2. Heat ghee along with jaggery in a pan. Add jeera and stir consistently till the mixture bubbles and thickens.
3. Pour into a greased flat steel plate. Flatten with a greased spatula.
4. When still warm, partially cut into square pieces before it cools and hardens.

TIKKADE (टिकड़े)

Ingredients:

½ cup Atta (whole-wheat flour)
½ cup Maida (refined flour)
2 tblsp. Refined oil
½ ball gurh (jaggery)
1 tblsp. sugar

Method:

1. Melt jaggery and sugar in 2-3 tablespoons of water.
2. Mix the atta and maida together and knead with refined oil first. Then add the sweet syrup gradually to form a stiff dough.
3. Roll with a belan to form into small circular shapes.
4. Deep fry in oil till light brown.

ZARDA (ज़र्दा)

(*A festive dish shared by Kamal Grover*)

Ingredients:

1 glass basmati rice
5 glasses water
Edible yellow colour (tip of a teaspoon)
Dry fruits (cashew nuts, almonds, walnuts)
Dry coconut chopped
6-7 green elaichi (cardamom) powdered
Kesar (saffron)a few strands
½ cup pure ghee (melted)
1 or ¾ glass sugar according to taste.

Method:

1. Boil 5 glasses of water. Add 1 glass of basmati rice into boiling water, add yellow colour. Cook till almost done but not fully.
2. Strain the rice in a sieve and immediately pour cold water over it. Drain out the water.
3. In a heavy bottom vessel pour 1 tablespoon pre-melted ghee and spread on the base of the vessel. (Do not put over the flame yet.)
4. Divide the rice into three portions. Layer the vessel as explained: 1st layer: Spread one portion of rice over the greased vessel. Over it spread one portion of sugar, dry fruit, sprinkle elaichi powder and saffron.

2nd layer: Repeat this layer with 1 tablespoon ghee, rice, sugar, dry fruit, elaichi powder and saffron in the same order as above.

3rd layer: This layer should have ghee, rice, dry fruit etc. with sugar right on top.

5. Cover vessel with a lid and cook on low flame for 30 minutes checking and stirring periodically.

Chapter 11

Home Remedies

(Age-old recipes handed down to Kamal Grover by her mother, Late Smt. Sham Devi Sachdeva, daughter of noted D I Khan Hakim Nathu Ram Sethi.)

CHAATA (चाटा)

(Treatment for cough)

Ingredients:

1 ½ tsp. honey
½ black elaichi (cardamom)
1 green elaichi (cardamom)
2 pepper corns
½ tsp ginger juice

Method:

1. Grind the cardamoms and pepper corns to a fine powder.
2. Heat a tawa and switch off flame.
3. Pour honey into a steel bowl and place over the tawa till slightly warm. (Do not heat honey on direct flame as it loses its efficacy).
4. Mix the powdered cardamoms and pepper into the warm honey along with ginger juice.

CHOONDI (चूँडी)

'Choondi' was a handy home cure for coughs which comprised a mix of powdered mishri (candied sugar) and powdered black elaichi (cardamom).

TREATMENT FOR COLD AND HEADACHE

(Serves as a curative and preventive if consumed regularly)

Ingredients:

250 gms Khus Khus (Poppy seeds)
250 gms Badam giri (Almonds)
250 gms Mishri (Candied sugar)
10 gms Green Elaichi (Cardamoms)

Method:

1. Grind each of the above ingredients separately in a mixie.
2. After grinding mix them together and store in an air-tight container.
3. Consume 2 tsps of the powder whenever required.

TREATMENT FOR PAIN AND UNEASINESS DUE TO FLATULENCE

Ingredients:

¼ tsp Ajwain (Carom seeds)
½ tsp Somf (Fennel seeds)
½ Black Elaichi (Cardamom)
1 Green Elaichi (Cardamom)
5-6 Pudina leaves (Mint)
1 cup water
Sugar as per taste.

Method:

1. Boil the ingredients in 1 cup water till the quantity reduces to ¼ cup. Add sugar and consume.

RELIEF FROM FLATULENCE

On a chakla or mortar and pestle grind a small piece of hing (asafoetida) with a few drops of water till a white paste forms. Dilute with water and apply around the navel.

(Note: *Not recommended in case of skin allergies.*)

RELIEF FROM INDIGESTION

Keep powdered black cardamoms in an airtight container. Consume a little quantity with sugar after a meal if suffering from indigestion.

FOR WAIST PAIN

Ingredients:

1 or 2 stems of Aloe Vera
2 tsps pure ghee
Turmeric, chillies and salt as per taste.

Method:

1. Peel Aloe Vera and cut very fine.
2. Heat ghee on a pan. Add aloe vera and spices. Saute and cover with a lid till cooked and dry.
3. Consume with a chapatti.

Chapter 12

Foot Prints of a Past

Dr. Dukhbhanjan Lal Sachdeva, Smt. Sham Devi Sachdeva,
Smt. Sarla Menon and Dr. M.K.K. Menon

Smt. Sarla Menon, daughter of Dr. Dukhbhanjan Lal Sachdeva and Smt. Sham Devi Sachdeva, remembers the spirit of bonhomie and close family ties in her joint family in Dera Ismail Khan. Baisakhi Mela was a much awaited four days event of festivities. Everyone would congregate at the Mela (fair) Ground. Each family would be seated in a circular formation spending the day together. They carried food from their homes as well as ate street food from the stalls set up. Each year they would get five salwar-kameez suits tailored for the occasion......a new set to be worn each day. The fifth set of clothes was reserved for wearing after a ritual bath in the Indus river. "As children we enjoyed the swings and merry-go-rounds which were set up. A professional photographer would also be in attendance clicking memorable moments."

Nani ghar, my maternal grandparent's home was a fun place where we would hang out most of the time since it was a large joint family with plenty of cousins to play with. My Nanaji, Hakim Nathu Ram Sethi, would tell us stories. We would seek his attention and inquire who was his favourite grandchild. His reply would be, "*Meydey vastey saarey hikka hin.*" (For me all are the same.) Having so many doting uncles and a grandfather, we collected coins and with our collection of three or four annas we would walk three miles to Gela Halwai's shop in Chhota bazaar and gorge on bhey pakorey, purni, samosa chaat and dahi bhalla. We were not allowed to venture alone to Barra Bazaar.

Our paternal home was in Toya Wala Mohalla on Sachdeva Street. Our house had four floors and from the topmost floor we could view the Indus river about three miles away. I studied at Arya Kanya Pathshalla where my Masi (aunt), Smt.Ghanshyam Devi, taught Sanskrit and was deputy Head Mistress. A weekly havan was held at school when we were required to wear a 'jogi' (saffron) colour dupatta. I recollect being slapped once by my head-mistress for forgetting to wear it. This did not go down well with me as a child and I still remember the unsavoury incident.

My elder sister's birth was received with a lot of joy that ladoos (sweets) were distributed to the neighbours. This treatment was not meted out to me as I was the second daughter. When six months old, I was given a 'malta' (citrus fruit) in my hands by Lalaji my paternal grandfather. Bhabhiji, my paternal grandmother used to say, "*Tehdey Daadey ne tehku malta ditha hai ke tehdey baad bhira paida theevey.*" (Your grandfather gave you a 'malta' so that you get a baby brother). Sure enough a brother was born after me and she would say, "*Aay bhira ghinn ayee hey*" (She has brought a brother).

Dr. Sat Prakash Sethi, better known as Ram, recollects, "Hakim Nathu Ram Street, was where our house was located. The street was named after my paternal grandfather, a noted Unani hakim of Dera Ismail

Khan. It was a known fact that he could diagnose a patient's ailment by a mere feel of the pulse. He practiced at Bhatia Bazaar where his shop was known as 'Hakim Nathu Ram di Hatti'. Besides herbal medicines he bottled herbal sherbets such as 'Rooh Parwar', 'Badam sherbet' and 'Gulab Ark' (Rose essence) which were sent to nearby Bannu and as far as Peshawar. He would often be accosted on his way by sick people who would request a treatment for their ailment. For such contingencies he carried some medicines, in his pouch, to be dispensed. He was a very spiritual person who converted the first floor of his house to a 'gurudwara' (prayer room). He had a premonition about his own death and requested all the members of his joint family to assemble at his first floor gurudwara for 'Sukhmani Sahib Paath' (prayers). Just as the prayers ended, his soul departed after three 'swas' (life breath). As a mark of respect to him all schools and shops of Dera Ismail Khan were shut. I was only eight years old when my father, Dr. Milap Chand Sethi, a renowned physician of Dera Ismail Khan, passed away at 39 years of age. He had been a brilliant medical student who not only topped Punjab University in his FSc examination but was a top ranker throughout his MBBS education at Lahore.

He had a clinic near Chhota Bazar where he had set up an X-Ray Plant too. His surgical skills were lauded by his own surgery professor at Lahore. All educational institutions and shops were closed as a mark of respect to him when he died. He was popular amongst both Hindus and Muslims. His Muslim friends outnumbered the former and they even came to our home to persuade us not to leave Dera Ismail Khan assuring us that we could never be harmed as we were Dr. Milap Chand Sethi's family. However, news about police atrocities on Hindus made our family uneasy and prompted us to bid adieu to our homeland."

"I was sent to Khalsa School along with my twin sibling, Lachhman, till class 5 primarily because my mother wanted us to learn Gurumukhi. After that we joined V.B. High School. Corporal punishment was very common at school. One day at class, a boy, who could not answer a question, was called to stand in front of the class. "Since I was the only one in the entire class who could answer, the teacher commanded me to smack the boy in front. I was put in a spot and obeyed the teacher by gently slapping my classmate's cheek. The enraged teacher barked, "This is not the way you smack. Let me show you how it is done." In a split second two mighty blows landed on my cheek. This was my reward for answering correctly." On another occasion our teacher expressed his disgust at a boy, who could not answer his question, by ruffling his well combed hair and remarking, सींधाँ करके आ वैन्दे हिन। आंदा वैंदा कख नई है। *Seendhaan karke aa vende hin. Aanda Venda kakh nai hay.* (He knows nothing beyond combing his hair.)

Hakim Sant Ram Sethi and Smt. Kako Bai Sethi

Dr. Neeraj Sethi's grandfather, Hakim Sant Ram Sethi, was part of a 'khandani' or family lineage of three generations of Unani hakims. His father was Hakim Nathu Ram Sethi who was the son of Hakim Khushi Ram Sethi whose father Shri Asa Ram Sethi may have been a hakim too but it is not certain. "My grandmother, Smt. Kako Bai would say that her father-in-law, Hakim Nathu Ram Sethi had '*shafa*' (healing touch) in his hands, was generous and used to treat the poor free"says Dr. Neeraj. "She had revealed that many 'seers'in weight of gold had been stored in earthen pots in the basement of their house where wheat was stored. Hakim Nathu Ram Sethi would personally prepare 'swarna bhasma', a medication using gold for patients who could afford it. My grandfather, Shri Sant Ram Sethi, had safely brought his trunk full of 'nuskhas' or Unani medicine formulations written in Urdu. Sadly, after his death, the papers were thrown away as no one realised their worth. Home cures were an inalienable part of our family regimen. For ear aches, warm mustard oil was poured into the ear and plugged with cotton wool. We used to have काड़ा 'kaada' (decoction) made of 'amaltas'(Laburnam) for a sore throat or cough. *Amaltas* seeds were boiled in water to form a concentrated liquid and consumed. My grandmother would cook delicious 'malpuas' and 'rabdi'. She would fondly say to her grandchild, ए ताँ मैडा नेहरू हे। *"Aay taan Meda Nehru hey."*

Rita Sethi, daughter of Shri Hari Krishan Sachdeva and Smt. Vidya Sachdeva, remembers her father saying that for one धेला 'dhela' they could buy a heap of pakoras along with a large free helping of भोर *bhor* (*pakora* crumbs) in D I Khan. More than the *pakoras* it was the free helping that children were drawn to. In British India an anna was equal to four (old) *paisas* and one *paisa* was equal to two *dhelas*. "These days it is rare to hear chaste Derewali spoken" says Rita. Her father's words, वंण गाल सुंण *"Vanrh gaal sunrh"*, still ring in her ears, although, she confesses how revolting it was to be addressed that way. Her maternal grandfather, Seth Bhoja Ram Malik, traded in whole-sale dry-fruits from Afghanistan and cloth besides being a financier in D I Khan. He had recovered from two business losses in his lifetime.....once when he was defrauded by his own cousins and a second time during the partition. After partition he re-established his wholesale cloth business from scratch in Chandni Chowk for which he was deeply indebted to a dear friend whom he had financed before partition. True to his word, the friend repaid the loan fully after the partition. "This act of honesty was so endearing that my grandfather regarded him as his third son."

Seth Bhoja Ram Malik was a pious man who would perform the '*Sharad Pitru Paksh*' ritual each year by inviting 50 pandits (Brahmins) to his house in Dera Ismail Khan. They would recite the Bhagwat Gita and 11 *gayatri mala jaap* (chanting). After prayers he would pay obeisance and touch their feet before feeding them a sumptuous meal comprising *saag* and *kheer* served in clay cups or *kasura*. He settled down in a spacious old traditionally built house in Karol Bagh. His 100 years old heritage home is occupied by his descendants. His daughter-in-law, a Punjabi from Amritsar, committed many a faux pas with Derewali, a language she was not familiar with. Sentences such as, (charcoal-brazier (*angeethi*) is getting lit) or हूला बख्ता पै "*Hoolla bakhta pey*"would make her smile. A boiling pot of milk overflowed as she could not understand what was being told to her, खीर वटींदा पै "*Kheer watinda pey*" (Milk is spilling). '*Kheer*' for her was a rice and milk dessert which she knew had not been prepared that day.

Kamal Grover reminisces her mother's words, "मैडी ताँ चुन्नी छिन-प्रुँण थी गई हे। "*Maidi taan chunni chhin-prun thi gai hay* (My dupatta has worn off.). She shares the predicament of her Bihari daughter-in-law who was non-plussed at meal-times when, in spite of a heap of chappaties at the table, family members would utter the word, 'ghinno' (घिन्नो) or take. She mistook it for 'ginno' (गिन्नो) or count and starved as she thought her intake of chappaties was being closely watched. While speaking of rotis she remembers that a piece of roti was called 'ghirai' (घिराई), half a roti called 'khanni' (खन्नी) and a quarter piece of roti was called, 'munni' (मुन्नी). Usage of the words was as below: मैकूँ खन्नी डे। or मैकूँ मुन्नी डे। *Makoon khanni de* or *Makoon munni de.*

Saroj Kumar shares an anecdote about her grandmother who was used to extinguishing the flame of the oil lamp or candle by briskly fluttering her dupatta. Old habits die hard that even when electric lights were introduced, the command, "बत्ती विस्मा डे"*Batti visma de* (Switch off the light.) saw her inadvertently follow the same practice. I remember my grandfather saying, "पैसे गूँडे विच पा डे।"*Paise goonde vich pa de* to his wife before going out. That meant, "Put some money into my coat pocket."

Swaran Palta, who lost her father, Shri Hakim Sachdeva, very early in life, was brought up by her uncle, Shri Tara Chand Sachdeva, popularly addressed as 'Malik Sahib'. My paternal grandmother, Smt. Dyali Bai, who was brought up in Khera Mohalla, would speak about a huge 'jhoola' (swing), in the 'aangan' (courtyard) of their house, which every new-born child of the family used as a tradition. When a child was born, a thick roti called, मोन टिक्की 'Mon Tikki', was prepared for the nursing mother. It was made of atta and lots of pure ghee. She would speak of 'borian' (sacks) of dry fruit being purchased for home consumption and about how she travelled, during partition, with jewellery concealed and tied around her waist.

Shri Mahesh Chander Sachdeva's early education in DI Khan began at home. His mother taught him Urdu alphabets which he wrote on an 18 ins.x 10 ins. wooden board or takhti which he would coat with a layer of *'gaachi'* or *Multani mitti* every day. It was hard work for a four year old to erase, coat the takhti and dry it for the next day. My uncle was obsessive about playfully tapping my head with his folded index finger. Sometimes it would hurt. He would say, ठूँगूरा खासें ताँ पैसा डेसाँ। *Thangura khaasen taan paisa desaan.* (Tolerate the tapping and I will give you a paisa.) My mother and grandmother would often object but to no avail. As I grew up my mother would laugh and say, ठूँगूरा खाके दिमाग तेज़ थी गया तैडा। *Thangura khake dimaag tez thi gaya taida.* (The knocks have sharpened your brain.) When angered, elders would call us खुरसानी खोता। (donkey from Khursan in Afghanistan). As DI Khan was on the trade route from Afghanistan frequent references to Afghan towns were cited in sayings and conversations.

The narrow lane or *galli* where we lived was flanked by houses on each side and a 'naala' or narrow drain flowed along the centre. In Derewali it was called चरी or 'chari'. The *dhobi* or washer-man was called चड़ोया or 'chadoya'. Our house had living rooms in front but deep in the far corner of the house was a dark room called, दूर-अन्दर or *'dur-andar'*. Family wealth was stored in this room. There was also an underground vault below the floor. While shopping it was customary to ask the vendor for an extra helping of anything ranging from vegetables, curd, milk or pakoras. The extra helping was called झूँगा or *'jhoonga'*. Shoppers would say, थोड़ा झूँगा पा डे। (Put some extra.)

I was just four when I viewed a mighty fire engulfing nearby villages from the third floor of our house. As disturbances became frequent, locals took advantage of the situation and resorted to looting. As a small boy I was horrified at the sight of salivating and foaming cattle being tied with ropes and ruthlessly stacked one atop the other on camel carts by looters. The cattle owners stood dazed and aghast as helpless bystanders. I remember accompanying my paternal grandmother and sister in a refugee train to India. We crossed the Indus river from DI Khan by steamer to Darya Khan from where we travelled in a train to Amritsar in August 1947. It was an inhuman and claustrophobic experience. My mother, baby sister and father, who was a physician, travelled by air as late as 1948. At the airport officials were preventing refugees from carrying valuables to India. Some people went to the extent of hiding ornaments inside parathas. My father had to prod my mother, who was carrying jewellery, to feign being sick and nauseous to escape the scrutiny.

Shri Subhash Chander Sachdeva related with glee his carefree boyhood days in DI Khan. "We took kite-flying very seriously and had competitions with our cousins who went to the extent of praying for victory, a day before, in the temple. We would personally prepare the 'manja' (string) with a coating of powdered glass, 'suresh' (glue) and black soot. We would play hockey and football in the grounds of the Company Bagh till the gardener would send us away. We were always up to some prank. I remember a time when we pulled down the sails of the boats anchored in the Sindh *dariya*. We were caught by the boat owners who wouldn't let us go until our teachers interceded. We would play 'guli danda' and marbles which we called 'चिडे' or *chidey* in Derewali. As children we looked forward to the *chhoti* and *barhi* Ramlila which were annual events. Our house had three floors. There was a rope attached to a wire basket or 'chhika' to lift things from the ground floor to the upper floors. The second floor had the puja room which we called the 'phulwadi.

I remember the temporary bridge made of boats joined together and leveled with planks placed on them during the winter months when the water in the river receded. This bridge extended for around 10 kms. across the entire breadth of the river from DI Khan to Daryakhan. Tongas could ply over the bridge with ease. Having studied till class 8 in DI Khan, I completed classes 9 and 10 at N.D. Victor High School in Jullundar cantonment and wrote my examination papers in Urdu. Having worn salwar-kurta all through school, I protested when forced to wear pants for college."

Rai Bahadur Chowdhury Ruchi Ram Khattar

Rai Bahadur Chowdhury Ruchi Ram Khattar was a prominent personality of Dera Ismail Khan. Besides being an entrepreneur and owner of the Khattar Electric Company, he was a member of the Legislative Assembly of the North West Frontier Province in 1937.

When the assembly seat fell vacant upon his passing away, Lala Tek Chand Dhingra was elected from Dera Ismail Khan (Rural) in November 1937.

Top: *Lala Sidhuram Dhingra*, Middle: *Lala Tek Chand Dhingra*, Front: *Yog Raj Dhingra*

Lala Tek Chand Dhingra, MLA and Freedom Fighter from Dera Ismail Khan

Shri Ashok Dhingra, son of Lala Tek Chand Dhingra, remembers DI Khan as a five year old. "My father's Estate had a dwarfed variety of khajur trees which bore very sweet fruit. The well in the estate was known as Bhammu Shah wala khu. Once when playing with friends we felt very thirsty, and drank water from the canal which was being fed from the 'khu' (well) by a 'rehat' or Persian wheel propelled by oxen. A bungalow owned by my father was occupied by the Collector of DI Khan district.

My father, Lala Tek Chand Dhingra, studied at the Mission School in DI Khan. During his teenage years in class 9 or 10 he was infused with patriotic fervour and persuaded all the students to wear clothes of khadi fabric to school. The Principal, a priest named Gayer Saab, was worried about the mental state of his students, who he thought, had fallen into wrong ways. He prayed for them to follow the right path. Nothing could deter my father. Years later when my father was elected MLA to the 1937 North West Frontier Province Legislative Assembly, his former principal Gayer Saab, residing in Peshawar, was proud of his accomplishment and sent him a lengthy telegram expressing how happy he was to hear the news and invited him to stay in his house whenever he visited Peshawar."

Lala Tek Chand Dhingra was a legendary freedom fighter, MLA and Chairman Public Accounts Committee. Influenced by Gandhiji's Non Cooperation Movement, Tekchand Dhingra left his government job and joined Lala Lajpat Rai's National College, Lahore, which was the hub of patriots like Bhagat Singh, Sukhdev and Jatin Das. He joined Lalaji's daily newspaper, 'Bande Mataram', as a staff reporter and became member of the Servants of the People Society. He actively participated in the Red Shirt movement of Khan Abdul Gaffar Khan and devoted his entire life to social causes."

When Netaji Subhash Chander Bose visited North-West Frontier Province he was accompanied by Kiron Das, younger brother of Shaheed Jatin Das who died in Lahore Jail on September 13, 1929 after fasting for 63 days. **Chander Dhingra**, youngest son of Shri Tek Chand Dhingra, says, "Kiron uncle told me that local women arranged and cooked food for guests from Bengal. I feel proud that our mother, Shanti Devi Dhingra, was among the group of women who met and served food to Netaji and Kiron Das. The latter always remembered with respect how supportive and protective my parents were towards him in Lahore especially during those difficult days when supporting a freedom fighter from Bengal meant incurring the wrath of the police force. My mother was lovingly called his 'Pathan Boudi' or Bhabhi.

Derewal groom, Chander Dhingra in Bengali attire at his wedding in 1981. Pic shows (Front) Shri Kiron Das (younger brother of Shaheed Jatindra Nath Das) and towering behind him, Shri Kultar Singh (younger brother of Shaheed Bhagat Singh.)

I had the opportunity to stay with Kiron Das uncle in Calcutta for three months in 1980. My Hindi book, 'Inqualabi Ke Saath Assi Din', is a memoir of days spent there and other stories of Lahore days of 1929 heard from him. For our family, he was an uncle and a guardian. As both my parents were no more, Kiron uncle and Kultar Singh uncle made it a point to be present for my wedding and to make up for their absence and honour their memory. It was their way to revive memories of Lahore days and their association with my parents. Kiron uncle wanted me to wear Bengali attire of Dhoti-Kurta for the day. It was, perhaps, abnormal for the relatives of the two families but many could see the hidden message behind it."

Rai Bahadur Sardar Hotu Singh Mongia

Rai Bahadur Sardar Hotu Singh Mongia's story is that of grit, hardwork and a brilliant intellect. Having lost his father at an early age, his mother educated him in an English medium school run by missionaries in Dera Ismail Khan. His headmaster was impressed by his remarkable capabilities that he employed him as a school teacher after he completed his higher education. Later, upon the headmaster's recommendation he entered government service and was commissioned in the Police. From thereon he rose like a phoenix to become District Judge,

Deputy Commissioner and Cabinet Minister of Revenue in the Royal Court of Indore[10], as a government appointee, in the reign of His Highness Maharajadhiraja Raj Rajeswar Sawai Shri Tukoji Rao Holkar Bahadur, G.C.I.E.

Some curious stories have travelled within the family over the years about when he killed a dreaded dacoit as well as an instance when he was poisoned by his enemies in Indore. He recovered but resigned and returned to his home town, Dera Ismail Khan. There was a street named after him in Lahore, RB Hotu Singh Mongia Street which, according to a family member, still exists. As District Judge his landmark judgements, pertaining to Customary Law, have been referred to in later cases. The book, "Customary Law of the Jullundar District" Vol 29 has been authored and compiled by Bhai Hotu Singh. He was conferred the title of Rai Bahadur[11] on the occasion of the Coronation Durbar in 1911 for his contribution to public services.

Sardar Sahib Jyot Singh Mongia, Secretary and Treasurer, Imperial Bank of India.

His sons, Sardar Gurmukh Singh Mongia and Sardar Jyot Singh Mongia did him proud by pursuing illustrious careers. The former as a lawyer and the latter as Secretary and Treasurer of the Imperial Bank of India. **Sardar Jyot Singh Mongia** completed his M.A. at Forman Christian College, Lahore and was a Fellow of the Royal Economic Society, Edinburgh University (Scotland). He started his career in the Finance Ministry of the government under the British rule. Thereafter he joined the Imperial Bank of India which became the State Bank of India in 1955. He headed the SBI headquarters in Calcutta and later in Delhi as Secretary and Treasurer.

Smt. Minnie Kandhari, his daughter, remembers him as a "good humoured and a deeply religious person who would start his day with one to two hours of prayers. He would donate generously to social causes without making a show of it. Although we lived in Lahore we spoke Derewali at home." She laughs as she recalls the 'sannu' (kitchen tongs) and the sentence, सन्नु नाल तैडा नक् नप्पां "*Sannu naal taida nak nappa*" (Should I grab your nose with kitchen tongs), मै तैडे वारी वन्या "*mai taide vaari vanna*" (You are worthy of my praise), मै तैडे मुड्डी वन्या "*mai taide muthi vanna*" (May you be blessed. Blessings were given with fists held on either side of the head).

Shri Sawan Singh Garkal and Smt. Vishni Devi Garkal (nee Bagai)

Smt. Pushpa Mata (nee Bagai) and Shri Jagdish Chander Mata.

Two sisters, **Vishni Devi Bagai** and **Pushpa Bagai** were born in a family of rich landowners. They were daughters of Rai Sahib Das Ram Bagai and were brought up in the palatial Bagai home where they witnessed large get-togethers and celebrations in their central 'aangan' (courtyard). The Bagais lived together as a joint family under one roof but with separate living suites and kitchens. Rai Sahib Das Ram Bagai lived on the ground floor while his father occupied the first floor. Vishni Devi ji studied till class 8 at the Arya Kanya Pathshalla in D I Khan and married Shri Sawan Singh Garkal, an affluent landowner and well-known barrister of Kohat. After marriage she became Smt. Vishni Devi Garkal. Her younger sister, Pushpa Bagai studied in Delhi and later in Mahila College, Lahore. She married Shri Jagdish Chander Mata, also from D I Khan, who specialised in sugar technology, worked in the sugar industry and set up his own enterprise in Gorakhpur (U.P.)

Shri Om Prakash Sachdeva, better known as Pretam, unravels a lucid account as an eight year old in DI Khan, "My first memory is of studying in a primary school and then a municipality school in a semi-rural setting in the outskirts of D I Khan. The school where my elder brother, Satish, and I studied had 99% Muslim boys. Apart from Urdu, Arabic was also taught there. As communal disturbances gathered momentum we were shifted to Victoria Biradri High School located on the road leading to the Company Bagh. After the fifth class exam I accompanied my elder brother and paternal grandmother to spend the summer vacations with my father who was posted in Jullundar. Little did we realise that we were not to return home again. My father, Capt. Thakur Das Sachdeva requested his Muslim army colleague in D I Khan to ensure our safe passage. There was great amity between Hindu and Muslim army officers even in those disturbed times. I remember visiting the Muslim colleague's home where his gracious wife offered us sherbet.

Photo taken in DI Khan one winter afternoon at the photographer's house in Sachdeva Street. (Left-Right): Smt. Shalo Bai, wife of Lala Gopal Das Sachdeva, Satish Kumar (Late Maj V.P. Sachdeva), Smt. Sham Devi, Pretam Lal (Shri O.P. Sachdeva, Mining Engineer) and Chandra. (Front): Shanti Swaroop (Dentist practising in Delhi) and Usha (Interior Designer). Potted plants are Badrinath Tulsi.

One fateful day in May 1947 we crossed the river Indus by a motorised launch to Daryakhan from where we travelled by train in 'intermediate-class' compartment. We passed through Lahore railway station which was absolutely deserted and reached Jullundar in the evening. My father received us and hired a tonga to take us to what would be our home, a large seven room house in Jullundar cantonment. My paternal grandfather, Lala Gopal Das Sachdeva, who had no intentions of leaving D I Khan, had to be persuaded to pack and leave. My father entrusted his good friend, Shri Jagdish Lal Gambhir, to ensure that grandfather left. Lala Gopal Das Sachdeva prepared for his journey by purchasing 20 steel trunks to pack his prized collection of Vedic books. He hired tongas for these to be transported to Daryakhan station by a steamer when the river was in full tide. He set out just before August 15, 1947 when most of D I Khan had been evacuated. The scene at Daryakhan railway station was not what grandfather had anticipated. Trains were packed with refugees like sardines till the roof. He was a lone figure on the platform refusing to depart without his trunks. Baloch militia were hovering nearby, eyeing the trunks and presuming them to contain valuables. Sensing trouble, Shri Gambhir bodily lifted grandfather and pushed him through the window of the train. While Gopal Das was fortunate, his elder brother, Govind Das Sachdeva's exit was tragic. He, too, was defiant about leaving his hometown but when he did he tried to take an alternative route via Bahawalpur thinking it to be safer. The train departed from Daryakhan but was halted at Bahawalpur. He was pulled out by two men who ruthlessly beheaded him with an axe. This scene was narrated by his travelling companion who had sneaked away and hopped into a goods train. My great grandfather, Rai Saheb Chela Ram Sachdeva had started the Khaji High School at his large estate in Bannu. He had an eminent tenure as the Agent, for the British Government, of this tribal region and was loved by the tribal lords for his honesty and sincerity in administering these wild areas. His exemplary administrative acumen earned him the title of Rai Sahib and a promotion as E.A.C. (Extra Additional Commissioner.) His testimonials, dating as far back as 1887, from Deputy Commissioners Mr F.D.Cunningham and Mr. Hutchinson are proof of his career progression. Although there is no documentation available, I was told by my father that Rai Sahib Chellaram was the first Indian to be posted as Deputy Commissioner of Gurgaon District. There is an interesting incident related by my grand mother who visited her father-in-law's house when he was posted in Gurgaon. As she sat in the lawns of his vast gable roofed bungalow she was threatened by a pack of monkeys who were aiming to attack her. An office peon, who was around, saved her by driving them away.

He later introduced himself to be one of the sons of the Last Mughal Emperor, Bahadur Shah Zafar.

Document dated 1889 tracing Rai Sahib Chela Ram's career.

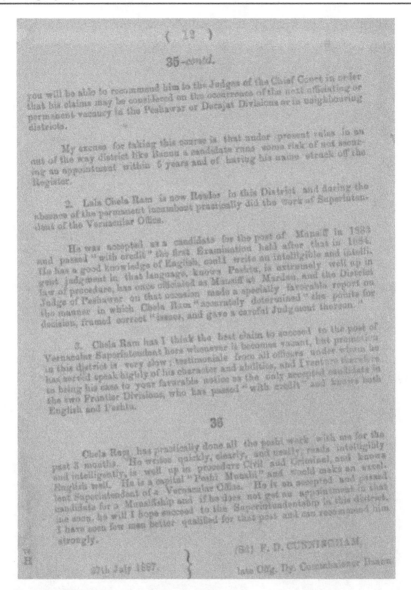

Document dated 1887 signed by Deputy Commissioner Bannu

Prior to joining the British-Indian Army in 1942 during World War II, my father worked as a science teacher for the State Education Department. I remember living in Abbottabad, a semi-hill station on the foot-hills of Kashmir with my Dad, Mom and brothers, Satish and Shanti Swarup.

Shri Thakur Das Sachdeva

I visited Bannu in summer as a child accompanied by my mother and Masi (maternal aunt). It was very cold even in that period. As late as February 1947 a letter written to my father by a relative, Ramlal Shiv Kumar, showed no inkling of the coming holocaust and the largest migration of human beings in the history of the world. The relative, in his letter, offered my father a lucrative proposal to invest in his wholesale trade of dry fruit export from Bannu.

A business proposal for investment in dry fruit

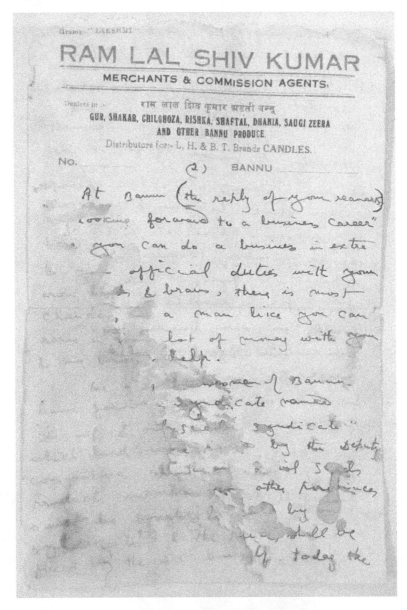

Business offer letter written in February 1947

My maternal great grandfather, Thariya Ram Dua, had a flourishing trade in Dacca muslin of which he sent ship-loads to Britain. From a prosperous man he was reduced to a state of penury overnight when his 'munshis' (clerks) in Dacca duped him with a lie that the ship carrying his cargo had sunk. Heart-broken, Shri Thariya Ram Dua, left home in D I Khan and lived the life of a recluse in an ashram on the banks of the river at Lahore, undivided India. After renouncing all worldly affairs and family ties, he rechristened himself as Swami Ramanand. The Swamiji never returned to his family and lived his remaining life at the Lahore ashram leading a saintly life. His wife lived with her son Lala Punnu Ram Dua, my Nana (maternal grandfather). I used to see her on our visits to my Nana's house, "A tall, fair, bent, neglected old lady sitting crouched on the floor against the wall, watching my Nani in the kitchen.

All we are left with today is a precious guidance for the family in the form of poetry/bhajan written by Swami Ramanand (Thariya Ram Dua). The bhajan was sung by him to my maternal uncle, Shri Ballabh Das Dua who had travelled all the way from Dera Ismail Khan to Lahore to seek his grandfather's blessings."

"गोविन्द विलास"
कृत रामानन्द स्वामी (Thariya Ram Dua)
प्यारे जान मनुष दा जनम औखा,
ईवें इसे नु न गवा मितर।
बड़े पुन जदंड़ जीव दे जमा होवन,
मिले जनम मनुष दा आ मितर।
अंग-अंग दे वल ध्यान कर रवाँ,
हिक अंग दा मुल तां पा मितर।
लख खर्चियाँ अंग न हिक मिल्दा
भावें पुछ सौदागराँ जा मितर।
हिक जनम, डूजी तंदरुस्ती,
तीजी अकल वी होवे सफा मितर,
चौथा इलम, नाले मिले नेक सौबत,
ईवें समां नां हर जा मितर।
तूँ तां आयों मुसाफ़राँ रात कटण
दुनिया विच जो मिसल सरां मितर।
गुज़रे रात परडेसियाँ कूच करसें,

होसी सुबह ज़रूर चल आ मितर
वांग रेल गाड़ी उमर सफ़र करेंदी,
नहीं इस नूँ ज़रा टिका मितर।
जीवें बाज़ बटेरे कूँ आ पकड़े,
तीवें मौत वी पकड़सिया आ मितर।
अचन चैत चलावसी चोट सिर ते
डेसी ख़बर न ज़रा सुना मितर
होसी सुबह ज़रूर चल आ मितर।

Transl. Knowing that being born as a human being is difficult
Do not waste away your precious life.
Only after accumulating many good deeds
Is a person born as a human-being.
Value the various parts of your body,
Try fixing a price on any one part.
Spending lakhs of rupees cannot procure a single body part,
Even if you were to approach a trader.
Foremost comes your birth as a human being and second is your health
Third is your intelligence clear and unwarped
Fourth is education alongwith good company.
Avoid wasting time if you possess these assets.
You have come only as a traveller to spend the night.
This world is like a 'serai' or inn.
As the night passes, you too will depart from this world,
But dawn will definitely break.
Just as a train, life moves on and on
Do not let it stop even for a moment.
Just as an eagle swoops down to prey upon a partridge,
Death too will swoop down upon you
All of a sudden without any warning.
The night will pass away like a stranger,
But day will surely dawn.

Chapter 13

Ode to Dera Ismail Khan

English translation of the poem,

मेरा डेरा इस्माइल खान: एक कहानीदार कविता - चंदर ढींगरा
(Published in 'Pahal' a Hindi literary magazine)

The poet Chander Dhingra was cradled in his mother's womb when she fled D I Khan in 1947.

MERA DERA ISMAIL KHAN

A narrative poem by Chander Dhingra
In an instant arose an unseen image,
At the mention of the word 'Dera'
Somewhere, in time, we too had a 'Dera',
We left behind amidst the bloodshed
Or ran away from it.

Obscured in the womb of my mother
I covered the distance unscathed,
But mother bore the brunt in body and mind
Brought about by our country's partition,
Shielded me from any blow
As I travelled rocking in comfort.

I had never seen you,
Why did you cling on to me
Every moment?
My entire life-time?

You were never mine
You were made for 'Ismail',
That 'Ismail' who moved on, too, in life's journey
And left behind those
For whom day dawned with the sunrise
For whom evenings blushed like a coy bride in all her splendour.

Ismail
Today let me speak candidly to you
You moved on
Leaving behind old ties.
Did you think?
Ties, like old buildings,
Will break apart one day?

Bonds don't easily snap
Nor are they erased with time.
I have a question for you
Having travelled together
Why did you drift away?
What was your dilemma?

Ismail
Wallowing in your constraints
Was part of your destiny.
It must have pained you
To carry the burden of your destiny?

Moving away from you
Mother was lonely
Often she would speak about
Her old haunts and neighbours
About seasons, about dry fruits
About rivers
And the usual things
Often seen by mothers
Around them.

I was close to her
While at play, I could hear her speak.
With a new question
I would give her a thread of thought.
And mother would soon begin a new story.

Today after years I think
Mother, perhaps, wished to impart much more
Through her stories and tales
About human relations and bonds
Maybe she wished to express about
The shifting face of humanity
Like the changing seasons.

Today after years
Mother's words unfold the truth
She would at times hesitate, at times hide.

Those kicked out of their home
Are left with pretensions and hesitation
Like two fake coins.
Mother's words settled in my mind
Like silt on the banks of a river.
All these years I wove
A spread of dreams
That Dera must be like this
That mother's neighbourhood must be like that
That Ismail must resemble that boy.

Maybe it is unbelievable to you
That just as people set sail in their boats of fancy,
Travelling the seven seas,
I too have delved in the world of fantasy
Roaming the streets of Dera Ismail Khan
Day dreaming
For several days, several times.

Ismail you would always say
This is our Dera
Not mine nor yours.
It's neither a country nor a land
It's a family.
Then why were we ousted
Mother and I, concealed in her womb,
From our family?
Why did you not come forward?
Why did you not show
The justice of the Pathans?

While fleeing from D I Khan
Mother tied a pouch
With some stuff
The stuff was made of dreams, of memories.

This pouch contained
The rising sun from the Sulaiman Mountain
Common to both the mothers,
Yours and mine.
Hidden inside this pouch
Was the mountain bordering Bannu
Sheikh Budin was its name
Remember, they would climb the mountain,
Your mother and mine,
To pray for favours.

You may have forgotten everything
But my mother kept these memories
Safe in her pouch
To pass on to me.
These were stories my mother wove
When she walked to the cross-road
Where people met.

These were stories that jolted her
With the mention of the place Quetta.
It was Quetta that buried
Beneath the debris of a building
Mother's near and dear ones.
Some almonds,
Some walnuts, some pine nuts were also there
Inside mother's pouch.
These she picked
While travelling from Bilot.

Mother studied only till class five
But she taught me lessons from history
How Punjab was divided the first time
How Layyah had been separated from Dera
How Kulachi and Tonk were left behind.

Mother would speak about Bohrianwalla Thalla
And Harmilapi ji.
About matters that meant not much to me
Mother was aware of it
That for a child such matters meant nothing.
Whether people went for *jandh, chola or janeyu* ceremonies
People would congregate from far off cities
And share their sorrows and grievances.

Maybe mother was relating stories
To lighten her burdens in a new land.
But, a new land in one's own country?
The very thought gave rise to angst.

Now years have passed
Since mother left us
I have visualised a home within my mind.
The sadness of mother's uprooted plight,
And through her stories my ties with you

Have become a burden
I have to carry my entire lifetime.

Ismail,
Our relations have scattered
Like beads snapped from a necklace.
Why don't we join them together
With the thread of faith, truth and courage.

Illustrations

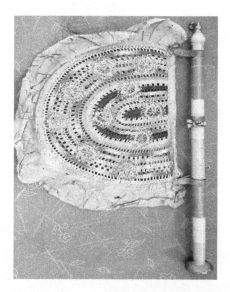

Hand-crafted Punkha with crochet work and zari.

Pathan headgear 'Kula' over which the turban or 'Lungi' is tied.

Karva, in silver, used for feeding milk to babies

Surmedani in silver contains kohl powder to beautify the eyes.

Wooden trinket box from D I Khan

Front: Langri (Brass vessel for pounding spices)
Back: Degchi (Cooking vessel in brass)

Wooden Sandook brought from D I Khan

Key to Shri Thakur Das Sachdeva's house in D I Khan

End Notes

1. 'Memories of Seven Campaigns' by James Howard Thornton, page.283

2. 'Frontier Folk of the Afghan Border and Beyond' (1920) by Lilian A. Starr, page 4

3. 'A German Staff Officer in India' by Count Hans Von Koenigsmarck. Authorised translation by P.H. Oakley Williams, page. 241

4. 'Sahib Log' by John Travers, published in 1910, page 44

5. 'Black Wood's Magazine Vol. CXCVII, Jan.-June 1915. Chapter, 'From the Outposts'. Pages.403, 404

6. Census of India 1911 Vol.13, pages 188, 190

7. 'Jeevan Ek Nidhi' by Devidayal Khanijou

8. 'Hamara Dera Ismail Khan-Tasveer-e Ashiana'by Shri Jaswant Ram Ailawadi, page 48

9. 'The Seraiki Language' by M. Bashir Ahmad Zami Bahawalpuri. English Translation by M. Jalal-ud-Din, page 10

10. 'Central India Agency' List No. 67, Part II (5) (a) (Govt. of India Publication Branch 1924)

11. Supplement To 'Who's Who in India' Popular Edition 1912. Page 107

CPSIA information can be obtained
at www.ICGtesting.com
Printed in the USA
LVHW011005260122
709187LV00003B/303

9 781638 865247